List of Contents

Introduction: The Path to Unleashing Your Career Potential

In a world filled with deadlines, responsibilities, and a constant, almost electric, drive for success, it's easy to lose sight of the essence of our careers—the very core that fuels our professional journeys. We often overlook the power of the mind and the incredible potential that lies within each of us. It's not surprising; in our race to reach the summit of our careers, we tend to navigate by the external compass, never truly charting the course within.

In this book, we'll defy the conventional wisdom that separates our professional lives from our personal selves. We'll embrace the idea that true career success is not a solo act, nor is it solely the result of hard work, opportunity, or sheer luck. It's also deeply intertwined with how we perceive ourselves, our goals, and the world around us. This isn't a story about job titles or corporate ladders. It's about unleashing the immense potential within you and redefining your journey to career fulfillment.

I understand the skepticism. The intersection of mindfulness and career success isn't a well-trodden path in the realm of professional literature. However, rest assured that the wisdom contained in these pages is not plucked from the clouds of abstract ideals. It's firmly grounded in science, research, and the lived experiences of countless individuals who, like you, have sought to transform their careers from ordinary to extraordinary.

Our journey begins with mindfulness, a practice that's often misconstrued as some ethereal, elusive concept—something reserved for spiritual gurus on mountaintops, far removed from the hustle and bustle of the professional world. In reality, mindfulness is an accessible and practical tool—a light guiding us through the labyrinth of our careers. It's about cultivating a state of awareness, an ability to be fully present in the here and now, and it's a skill that can be harnessed by anyone.

Consider your daily work life—filled with meetings, deadlines, emails, and responsibilities. How often do you find your thoughts scattered, your mind racing, and your actions on autopilot? The power of mindfulness is in its capacity to anchor you in the present moment, helping you regain control of your thoughts and actions. This isn't about discarding ambition or relinquishing the pursuit of success. It's about ensuring that your journey is rooted in intention and clarity.

When you're mindful, you can navigate the corporate maze with a keen understanding of your own values and aspirations. You become adept at deciphering between mere busyness and meaningful action. Mindfulness isn't a magic wand that grants instant promotions or substantial raises, but it equips you with the inner wisdom to make choices that truly resonate with your career goals.

Now, let's talk about affirmations—a concept often underappreciated in professional discourse. At their core, affirmations are about self-empowerment and a declaration of your intent. They serve as powerful instruments in transforming your mindset, cultivating self-belief, and instilling the conviction that you're capable of achieving greatness.

But, and it's an important "but," affirmations alone are not a shortcut to success. They're not incantations that magically manifest your desires. Affirmations work in tandem with mindfulness, acting as a catalyst for change when coupled with deliberate, focused action. When you harness the force of affirmation in your career journey, you sculpt a mental landscape that reflects the direction you wish to pursue.

It's about silencing the inner critic—the voice that often tells you that you're not good enough, not qualified enough, or not deserving of your goals. With affirmations, you'll have a tool to challenge these negative narratives, replacing them with statements that reflect your true potential. As you repeat these affirmations, your subconscious begins to accept them as truths, altering your self-perception and driving actions that align with your aspirations.

This book is a roadmap for your career transformation, and its principles are drawn from the insights and wisdom of countless professionals who have undergone their unique metamorphoses. It's a collection of practical strategies and exercises that are designed to create a harmonious synergy between your inner self and your professional goals.

We'll uncover how to employ mindfulness in enhancing your communication skills, fostering meaningful relationships, and embracing leadership that resonates with your core values. We'll explore the remarkable power of affirmations in bolstering your confidence, promoting resilience, and steering your career toward its zenith.

The adventure that lies ahead isn't about the quick fix or the easy route; it's about a deep, personal transformation—the kind that lasts a lifetime. It requires your active participation, dedication, and an unwavering belief in your own potential.

Prepare to start a exploration that will not only transform your career but also lead to a profound reconnection with your true self.

Chapter 1: The Power of Mindfulness

1.1: Understanding Mindfulness

In a world defined by constant motion and ceaseless noise, the concept of mindfulness offers a sanctuary of serenity and the promise of personal and career growth. It is not a magical incantation or a mystical ritual but a simple yet profound practice rooted in a deeper understanding of self, thought, and emotion. To grasp the significance of mindfulness, we must first embark on a journey of definition, exploration, and the revelation of its scientific underpinnings.

Defining Mindfulness and Its Role in Personal and Career Growth

Mindfulness is an ancient art, but its relevance in our fast-paced, modern lives is more poignant than ever. At its core, mindfulness is the practice of being fully present in the moment, observing one's thoughts and feelings without judgment. It's about stepping away from the ceaseless stream of mental chatter and immersing oneself in the richness of the present. Mindfulness is not a wholesale rejection of the past or an all-consuming obsession with the future; it's an artful combination between acknowledging the past's lessons and preparing for the future while savoring the present.

In the context of personal and career growth, mindfulness becomes a powerful ally. When we practice mindfulness, we become keenly aware of our thoughts and emotions. This heightened awareness allows us to break free from the shackles of unexamined assumptions, patterns, and reactions. We gain insight into our motivations, desires, and fears, enabling us to make conscious choices that are in alignment with our true selves.

Imagine the impact of this in your career. Instead of operating on autopilot, driven by societal expectations or external pressures, you become the architect of your professional path. Mindfulness enables you to identify your core values, passions, and strengths. It empowers you to set meaningful career goals based on an authentic understanding of what truly matters to you.

Mindfulness also plays a pivotal role in decision-making. In the cacophony of life, we often make choices haphazardly, driven by fleeting impulses or the desire to conform. Mindfulness allows us to pause, to sift through the noise, and to listen to our inner compass. It fosters the discernment to choose career paths that resonate with our essence, rather than being swayed by superficial allure.

Furthermore, mindfulness is an antidote to the epidemic of stress and burnout that plagues many professionals. It equips you with the tools to navigate the stormy seas of a demanding career with grace. In times of pressure, the ability to step back, observe your thoughts, and manage your responses becomes invaluable. It offers a reprieve from the relentless grip of stress and a pathway to balance and well-being.

The Science Behind Mindfulness and Its Benefits

If mindfulness seems like an abstract concept, its scientific underpinnings provide concrete evidence of its efficacy. Neuroscientists have delved into the intricacies of the brain to unravel the profound impact of mindfulness on our cognitive functions, emotional regulation, and overall well-being.

One area of the brain that bears the imprints of mindfulness practice is the prefrontal cortex, often referred to as the brain's "CEO." This region is responsible for high-level functions such as decision-making, attention, and impulse control. Regular mindfulness practice has been shown to enhance the activity and connectivity of the prefrontal cortex. In practical terms, this means that mindfulness bolsters your cognitive abilities, enabling you to make wiser decisions, focus more effectively, and manage impulses skillfully.

Mindfulness also exerts a calming influence on the amygdala, the brain's emotional center. This small but potent almond-shaped structure is the epicenter of our emotional responses, particularly fear and stress. Research demonstrates that mindfulness meditation can reduce the amygdala's reactivity to emotional stimuli. As a result, practitioners of mindfulness exhibit enhanced emotional regulation, allowing them to respond to challenges with equanimity rather than knee-jerk reactions.

The benefits of mindfulness extend beyond the realm of neuroscience. Studies have shown that regular mindfulness practice can lower blood pressure, improve immune function, and enhance overall physical health. The mind-body connection is a potent force, and mindfulness serves as a bridge between the two. When you cultivate mindfulness, you're not merely nurturing your mental landscape but also tending to your physical well-being.

The application of mindfulness principles in a professional setting is particularly striking. Studies have indicated that individuals who incorporate mindfulness into their work routines report lower levels of stress, increased job satisfaction, and improved interpersonal relationships. They are better equipped to handle the demands of a high-stakes career without succumbing to the corrosive effects of chronic stress. Mindfulness is not just a soft skill; it is a transformative tool that sharpens the edge of your professional performance.

Real-Life Success Stories Through Mindfulness
To appreciate the transformative power of mindfulness, one need not look further than the stories of those who have harnessed its potential to achieve personal and career success.

Consider the case of Sarah, a mid-level manager in a fast-paced tech company. Her days were a frenetic whirlwind of meetings, deadlines, and an ever-expanding inbox. The constant pressure took a toll on her physical and emotional health. Sarah decided to explore mindfulness as a means of finding balance amidst the chaos.

Through regular mindfulness practice, she developed a profound sense of self-awareness. She recognized that her relentless pursuit of perfection was a source of unnecessary stress. With this insight, she embraced a more compassionate approach to her work and herself. She set boundaries, delegated tasks, and, most importantly, learned to let go of the need for constant control. The result was not just a reduction in stress but also a significant improvement in her leadership skills. She fostered a more collaborative and innovative team environment, which ultimately propelled her career to new heights.

John, an entrepreneur on the verge of burnout, also discovered the potency of mindfulness. His small startup was experiencing rapid growth, but the pressure was taking a toll on his well-being. John's journey into mindfulness began as a quest for stress management but soon evolved into a transformative career strategy.

As he delved deeper into mindfulness practices, he realized that he had been approaching business challenges with tunnel vision. Mindfulness allowed him to see the bigger picture. He became attuned to emerging market trends and discovered creative solutions to business hurdles. In essence, mindfulness expanded his entrepreneurial vision. John's company not only survived but thrived, and his story became a testament to the profound impact of mindfulness on career success.

These stories, while unique, share a common thread: mindfulness is not a whimsical notion but a pragmatic path to personal and career growth. It is a wellspring of resilience, insight, and empowerment. The science and the stories together affirm that mindfulness is not a nebulous concept but a tangible tool for navigating the complexities of the modern professional world.

1.2: Techniques for Mindfulness

In a fast-paced world brimming with professional commitments, personal responsibilities, and the constant buzz of information, it's easy to get swept away by the turbulence of life. We often find ourselves ricocheting from one task to another, rarely stopping to catch our breath. In this relentless pursuit of our goals and ambitions, we might inadvertently neglect one of the most potent tools we have for personal transformation and professional growth: mindfulness.

Mindfulness is not just a buzzword or a trendy practice; it's a profound way of engaging with the world and our own inner landscapes. It's an art of being present, of embracing the current moment with a sense of curiosity and non-judgmental awareness. In the context of career development and personal growth, mindfulness serves as a beacon guiding us toward success. Submerging ourselves in the depths of mindfulness can be akin to peering into a crystal-clear pond where the reflection of our true potential becomes vividly apparent.

Exploring Different Mindfulness Techniques

Mindfulness is a multi-dimensional collections of techniques, each offering a unique path toward the same destination—awareness and self-realization. Some might find solace in the rhythm of their breath, while others turn to mindfulness meditation. There's no one-size-fits-all approach, which is one of the beautiful aspects of this practice.

1. Mindfulness Meditation: At its core, mindfulness meditation is a practice of undistracted focus, commonly on the breath or a chosen object. It's an invitation to notice thoughts and sensations as they arise, without attachment or judgment. As you sit in stillness, you may discover a profound connection with your inner self. Through this technique, the ceaseless stream of thoughts gradually transforms into a tranquil river, offering clarity and peace.

2. Body Scan: The body scan technique involves systematically shifting your awareness from one part of your body to another, observing sensations, tension, or discomfort. By paying close attention to physical sensations, you develop a heightened awareness of how your body responds to stress and stimuli. It's like tuning into the orchestra of your body, understanding its symphony of responses.

3. Walking Meditation: In our quest for career success, we often overlook the simple act of walking. Walking meditation is a practice of slow, deliberate steps. As you walk, you focus on the sensation of each step, the movement of your body, and the connection between your

feet and the earth. It's a practice that unites your mind with your physical presence, grounding you in the present moment.

4. Breathing Techniques: Mindful breathing is a cornerstone of mindfulness practice. It's as simple as paying attention to your breath—its rhythm, depth, and the rise and fall of your chest. By directing your awareness to the breath, you anchor yourself in the here and now. It's an anchor that can prevent you from being swept away by the tides of stress and anxiety.

Practical Steps for Incorporating Mindfulness into Daily Life

While these mindfulness techniques provide various entry points into the world of mindfulness, it's essential to emphasize that mindfulness isn't limited to sitting in meditation for hours on end. It's a versatile practice that can seamlessly integrate into your daily life, infusing every moment with clarity and presence.

1. Mindful Morning Routine: Begin your day with intention and mindfulness. As you wake up, take a moment to appreciate the comfort of your bed, the warmth of your blanket, and the sensation of stretching your body. When you eat breakfast, do so with complete attention to the flavors and textures. As you shower and dress, notice the water on your skin and the sensation of clothing against your body. By weaving mindfulness into your morning routine, you set a positive tone for the day ahead.

2. Mindful Work Environment: Whether you're in an office, a home office, or any other work setting, it's possible to create a space that supports mindfulness. Arrange your workspace to minimize distractions. Practice mindful breathing between tasks, allowing yourself a few moments of stillness to reset and refocus. Engage fully with the task at hand, and you'll find that your productivity and creativity flourish.

3. Mindful Eating: In our rush to achieve career goals, we sometimes consume our meals absentmindedly. Mindful eating is an opportunity to savor the flavors, textures, and nourishment that food provides. As you eat, pay attention to each bite, appreciating the effort that went into preparing your meal. This practice not only enhances your connection with your food but also helps maintain a healthy relationship with eating.

Overcoming Common Challenges in Practicing Mindfulness

While mindfulness can be a transformative force, it's not immune to challenges. The very nature of our busy lives often clashes with the intention to stay present. Here are some common hurdles and strategies for overcoming them:

1. Restless Mind: Your mind may resist settling into mindfulness. It's normal for thoughts to continue racing during your practice. The key is not to judge or suppress these thoughts but to acknowledge them and gently return your focus to your chosen anchor, such as the breath.

2. Lack of Time: Finding time for mindfulness in a packed schedule can be challenging. Start small. Even a few minutes of mindfulness each day can make a difference. Over time, you can gradually increase the duration of your practice.

3. Impatience: It's common to expect quick results. Mindfulness is a journey, not a destination. The benefits may not be immediately evident, but with persistence, you'll notice positive changes in your mindset and well-being.

4. Distractions: Life is filled with distractions, from technology to external noises. Instead of battling these distractions, use them as opportunities for mindfulness. Notice the sound of birds chirping, the feel of your fingers on a keyboard, or the taste of your coffee.

As you navigate the many techniques and strategies of mindfulness, you'll find that it's not a destination to reach but a lifelong path to explore. It's an adventure that can lead you to deeper self-awareness, enhanced focus, and a profound transformation that can greatly influence your career success and personal growth.

1.3: Mindfulness and Career Success

In a world where the demands of work and life can become a tempest, the concept of mindfulness emerges as the lighthouse guiding us through turbulent waters. It's a beacon that, when embraced with intention and commitment, has the potential to transform our professional lives. In this subchapter, we delve into the profound impact mindfulness can have on your career success. We'll explore how this practice enhances your ability to focus, make informed decisions, and maintain a harmonious balance between your work and personal life.

How Mindfulness Can Enhance Focus and Decision-Making

Imagine a scenario: You're at your desk, buried under a mountain of reports, emails, and impending deadlines. Your mind, like a pinball, ricochets between tasks. You feel pressure mounting and decision fatigue creeping in. This is a familiar tableau for many in the modern workforce. It's a challenging landscape to navigate, but here's where mindfulness emerges as a trusted ally.

Mindfulness is about the cultivation of presence—the ability to anchor your awareness in the here and now. By focusing your attention on the task at hand, you tap into a state of heightened clarity. It's not about bulldozing through your to-do list; it's about savoring each moment, each task, and each interaction.

Through mindfulness, you build the capacity to approach tasks with a sense of calm and purpose. This is where the magic happens. It's akin to fine-tuning a radio, finding that clear frequency, and experiencing the symphony of life without interference.

But let's be clear: this isn't about perfection. Your mind will still wander; distractions will persist. Mindfulness doesn't eliminate these challenges, but it arms you with the tools to gracefully guide your focus back to the present. By doing so, you enhance your decision-making.

Imagine making pivotal career choices with a clear mind. You're no longer shackled by the maelstrom of anxieties or the burdens of past mistakes. Mindfulness, in its essence, is a method of rewiring your response to stress and pressure. You can ponder complex questions and confront dilemmas with a composed mind.

Mindful decision-making isn't solely about logic; it's also about intuitive wisdom. When you're in the moment, deeply attuned to your surroundings and emotions, you tap into a wellspring of insight. It's that gut feeling, that inner voice, guiding you toward the path that aligns with your authentic self.

Balancing Work and Life with Mindfulness
The modern world has a peculiar habit of demanding our undivided attention, both at work and in our personal lives. Juggling these dual responsibilities can feel like walking on a tightrope strung between skyscrapers. The very concept of work-life balance has become a topic of perennial discussion.

In this complex landscape, mindfulness emerges as the fulcrum upon which this balance is achieved. When you're mindful, you're fully present wherever you are. At work, you're immersed in the tasks at hand, making the most of your professional time. At home, you're engaged with your family and personal pursuits.

One of the greatest misconceptions about mindfulness is that it necessitates a significant time investment. In reality, it's about the quality of moments, not the quantity. You can introduce mindfulness into your daily life without lengthy meditation sessions or elaborate rituals.

Consider your daily commute. For many, it's a routine fraught with frustration and impatience. But it could also be an opportunity for mindfulness. Rather than cursing traffic jams or crowded trains, you can use this time to center yourself. Take a deep breath and be fully aware of the sights and sounds around you. It's a small adjustment that transforms a potentially stressful experience into a mindful interlude.

This same principle can be applied at work. Instead of fretting about the never-ending to-do list, consider practicing mindfulness during short breaks. Step away from your desk, close your eyes, and focus on your breath. You'll be amazed at how this simple act can reinvigorate your energy and clarity.

Balancing work and life through mindfulness isn't a zero-sum game. It's not about rigidly partitioning your day into professional and personal spheres. Instead, it's about integrating mindfulness into every moment, ensuring that your career and personal life coexist harmoniously. It's not an either-or scenario; it's an "and" that weaves both aspects of your life together.

Achieving Mindfulness at the Workplace

The workplace can often resemble a bustling metropolis, with the cacophony of ringing phones, buzzing emails, and hurried footsteps. It's easy to get swept up in this frenetic pace. However, it's precisely in this milieu that the power of mindfulness shines brightest.

Mindfulness at the workplace is about reclaiming your center amidst chaos. It's like a serene island amidst the turbulent seas. It doesn't require you to flee to a monastery; instead, it's about creating pockets of stillness in your workday.

Start your day with intention. Rather than diving headlong into your emails, spend a few moments in contemplation. Take a deep breath and set your intention for the day. What are your priorities? What is the emotional tone you want to bring to your interactions? This simple act can transform your entire workday.

Then there are those micro-moments, the breathers between meetings or tasks. In the rush to be perpetually productive, we often overlook these intervals. Mindfulness encourages you to make the most of them. You can do a brief body scan, grounding yourself in the physical sensations of the moment. Or you can take a short walk, appreciating the world outside your office window. These tiny islands of mindfulness are like oases in the desert of busyness, revitalizing your focus and presence.

And let's not forget about the mindfulness of communication. In a professional setting, we engage in countless conversations—some brief, some lengthy.

Mindful communication means being fully present when you're interacting with a colleague, supervisor, or subordinate. It's about listening not just with your ears but with your whole being. It's acknowledging the person in front of you and responding with empathy.

Mindfulness in the workplace isn't about idleness or disengagement. In fact, it's quite the opposite. It's about harnessing your mental faculties to the fullest, ensuring that your professional contributions are marked by presence, clarity, and authenticity.

Chapter 2: Harnessing the Power of Affirmations

2.1: Introduction to Affirmations

In the our professional lives, there exists a potent thread that often goes unnoticed – the art of affirmations. At first glance, they may seem like mere words strung together, but in reality, affirmations are the silent architects of our thoughts and actions. These deceptively simple phrases have the power to shape the narrative of our careers, directing our focus towards a future we desire and crafting a mindset resilient enough to weather the storms of uncertainty and ambition. In this chapter, we'll embark on a journey into the world of affirmations, unlocking their potential to propel us to the zenith of our careers.

What Are Affirmations, and Why Do They Matter for Your Career?

Affirmations, in essence, are concise, positive statements that resonate with your deepest aspirations. They serve as verbal declarations of your goals, values, and strengths. These declarations may seem like whispers in the cacophony of professional life, but they possess a unique and profound power. Affirmations function as beacons guiding your internal dialogue, steering your thought patterns, and influencing your actions. They may not magically transform your circumstances, but they can metamorphose the lens through which you perceive and react to those circumstances.

Affirmations matter for your career because they have a direct influence on your belief system and, consequently, your behavior. Imagine affirmations as the rudder of a ship navigating through the tumultuous sea of your professional journey. They steer the course, providing direction and purpose. By consistently reinforcing positive and empowering beliefs about yourself and your capabilities, affirmations empower you to overcome self-doubt and adversity. They become the compass guiding your choices, and as a result, your career trajectory.

Think of the last time you faced a daunting career challenge or embarked on a new venture. In such moments, our inner dialogue can sway between optimism and doubt. This internal conversation, driven by our core beliefs, influences how we tackle opportunities and setbacks. Affirmations offer a method to tip the balance toward optimism and resilience.

The key to understanding the importance of affirmations in your career lies in recognizing the symbiotic relationship between beliefs and actions. When you wholeheartedly believe in your abilities, you're more likely to take action, seek opportunities, and persevere. Affirmations act as catalysts for cultivating these unwavering beliefs, helping you confront challenges, achieve milestones, and evolve as a professional.

The Psychological Mechanisms Behind Affirmations
To comprehend the profound impact of affirmations, it's crucial to delve into the intricate workings of the human

psyche. The mind is an intricate threads of thoughts, beliefs, and emotions, constantly weaving its way through the experiences that shape us. Within this area, our subconscious mind plays a pivotal role.

Affirmations have their roots in the subconscious mind, the silent guardian of your beliefs and self-perception. This part of your psyche operates beneath the surface, silently absorbing the information and experiences that mold your perception of the world and, more importantly, yourself. Affirmations are the means through which you consciously communicate with this silent guardian, introducing new beliefs and perspectives.

Our subconscious mind doesn't distinguish between reality and imagination; it accepts the information we provide as the truth. This is where the power of affirmations emerges. When you repeatedly affirm your capabilities, resilience, and potential for success, your subconscious mind internalizes these declarations as factual. It adjusts its narrative to align with your affirmations, thereby influencing your self-esteem, self-worth, and confidence.

In the realm of psychology, the self-fulfilling prophecy is a phenomenon that validates the potency of affirmations. This theory asserts that the beliefs we hold about ourselves manifest in our behaviors, ultimately influencing the outcomes we experience. Affirmations act as the creators of self-fulfilling prophecies. When you consistently affirm your ability to thrive in your career, your actions align with this belief, increasing the likelihood of your success. The psychological mechanisms at play here are akin to setting your internal compass to navigate toward prosperity and fulfillment.

Using Affirmations to Reprogram Your Mindset
Now, let's delve into the practicality of affirmations. To harness their transformative power, you must engage in a deliberate process of reprogramming your mindset. This process involves crafting and adopting affirmations that resonate with your career aspirations and values.

Start by identifying the areas of your career where you may be grappling with self-doubt, fear, or negative self-talk. Perhaps it's the imposter syndrome that occasionally creeps in, casting shadows of self-questioning. Or maybe it's the anxiety that accompanies stepping out of your comfort zone. These are the spaces where affirmations can weave their magic.

Affirmations should be framed in the present tense, as if they are already true. For example, if you're battling imposter syndrome, your affirmation might be: "I am a skilled professional who adds value to every project I undertake." By stating it as a present reality, you trigger your subconscious mind to embrace this belief.

Consistency is key. Repetition is the engine that drives the reprogramming process. Make it a daily ritual to recite your affirmations, preferably in the morning or before significant career milestones. The more you declare these positive truths about yourself, the more they become woven into the fabric of your self-concept.

Moreover, anchoring your affirmations in specific actions can accelerate their impact. If your affirmation relates to improved leadership skills, accompany it with a plan to attend leadership workshops or seek mentorship. Action bolsters the belief system, transforming affirmations into tangible career growth.

Affirmations are not a quick fix, but they are a potent and accessible tool to recalibrate your mindset. By consistently engaging in this practice, you embark on a journey of self-discovery and empowerment, redefining your career narrative from one of self-doubt to one of self-assuredness and achievement.

2.2: Crafting Effective Affirmations

In the quest for career success and personal fulfillment, we embark on a journey filled with challenges, uncertainties, and sometimes, our own internal doubts. The mind, a powerful instrument, can either be our greatest ally or our most formidable adversary. What if I told you that within the realm of your thoughts lies the key to unlocking your true potential and achieving your career goals? This is the magic of affirmations, a mental tool that, when wielded with precision, can pave the way for remarkable transformation.

Writing Affirmations That Resonate With Your Career Goals

Affirmations are more than just positive words strung together; they are declarations of intent that harness the energy of your mind and spirit to propel you toward your desired destination. Crafting effective affirmations is an art, and like any art, it requires attention, intention, and a profound connection to your objectives.

To craft affirmations that resonate with your career goals, it's essential to begin with a clear vision of what those goals are. Clarity is the compass that will guide you through this journey. If you seek a promotion, a career change, or simply a more rewarding job experience, take a moment to reflect on the specifics of your aspirations. What does your ideal career look like? What responsibilities, challenges, and rewards do you envision? It's this clarity of purpose that forms the foundation of effective affirmations.

Once you've clarified your career objectives, your affirmations should be tailored to mirror these intentions. For instance, if your goal is to secure a leadership role, you might craft an affirmation such as, "I am a confident and influential leader who inspires and guides my team to success." Note that the affirmation is not merely about the end goal; it also embodies the qualities and attributes necessary to attain it. "Confident" and "influential" are traits that you aim to nurture within yourself.

Incorporate the present tense into your affirmations. Rather than stating, "I will become a successful entrepreneur," affirm, "I am a successful entrepreneur." This linguistic shift is not about denying the present reality but about affirming your commitment to manifesting the future you desire.

Tailoring Affirmations to Your Unique Aspirations
As you craft affirmations, remember that one size does not fit all. Each of us embarks on a distinct career path, shaped by our unique skills, interests, and experiences. Therefore, your affirmations should be as unique as your aspirations.

Begin by identifying your strengths and attributes. What sets you apart? Do you possess exceptional problem-solving skills, a talent for creative thinking, or a knack for building strong relationships with colleagues and clients? Your affirmations should celebrate these strengths and reinforce your belief in them.

For example, if your strengths lie in your creativity and innovation, an affirmation might read, "I am a creative thinker who brings fresh and valuable ideas to every project." This affirmation not only acknowledges your unique talents but also reaffirms your commitment to showcasing them in your career.

Affirmations can also be tailored to address areas where you desire growth. Perhaps you recognize that you need to enhance your leadership skills, your ability to manage stress, or your communication capabilities. Crafting affirmations that address these growth areas can be transformative. "I am becoming a resilient and effective leader" or "I am developing excellent communication skills" can serve as powerful daily reminders of your ongoing personal and professional development.

Turning Negative Self-Talk into Positive Affirmations

We all grapple with self-doubt and negative self-talk from time to time. In the world of career and personal growth, these inner critics can be particularly relentless. The power of affirmations extends to silencing the naysayers within.

Negative self-talk often manifests as limiting beliefs. Phrases like "I'm not good enough," "I'll never make it," or "I don't deserve success" can plague the mind and impede progress. However, each of these negative beliefs can be reframed into a positive affirmation that redirects your thinking.

For instance, if you often find yourself doubting your abilities, transform "I'm not good enough" into "I possess valuable skills and continually improve them." By doing so, you pivot from self-criticism to self-empowerment. The new affirmation acknowledges your capabilities while inspiring a growth mindset.

Likewise, "I'll never make it" can be replaced with "I am on a path of constant progress and success." This shift in language reminds you that success is a journey, not a fixed destination. It encourages perseverance and resilience.

Affirmations provide a formidable defense against the destructive forces of self-doubt and negativity. They remind you of your potential and reinforce the idea that your career goals are within reach.

When crafting effective affirmations, remember this: the more personal and specific your affirmations are, the more profound their impact. They serve as your daily companions on your career journey, reinforcing your beliefs, clarifying your intentions, and silencing the doubts. Through the power of your mind, and with the right affirmations, you'll embark on a transformative path toward achieving your career aspirations.

2.3: Integrating Affirmations into Daily Life

In the journey toward career success, we've explored the profound influence of affirmations on our mindset and belief systems. We've seen how these carefully crafted, positive statements can be pivotal in reshaping our attitudes and bolstering our self-esteem. But understanding the theory is just the beginning; the real magic lies in the application. In this subchapter, we're going to delve deeper into the practicality of affirmations and discuss their seamless integration into your daily life.

Creating a Daily Affirmation Routine

Affirmations aren't mere words; they're intentions that require daily nurturing. Crafting a daily affirmation routine can be likened to tending to a garden. Just as a gardener diligently waters and cares for their plants, you must nurture your affirmations daily to witness the blossoming results in your life. Here's how you can create and maintain a daily affirmation routine that aligns with your career aspirations.

Morning Rituals: Start your day with affirmations. Before the whirlwind of emails, meetings, and deadlines, take a moment to focus on yourself. Find a quiet space, close your eyes, and recite your chosen affirmations. These affirmations should align with your career goals. For example, if you're striving for a promotion, you might repeat, "I am confident and capable of achieving my career goals."

Visual Aids: Visual reminders can be exceptionally powerful. Consider placing your chosen affirmations on sticky notes, which you can post on your bathroom mirror, your desk, or the dashboard of your car. These serve as subtle nudges throughout the day, gently steering your thoughts in the right direction.

Midday Reset: At the midpoint of your workday, take a short break to reinforce your affirmations. This might involve stepping outside for some fresh air and repeating your affirmations in your mind. The break not only reenergizes you but also reinforces your positive mindset.

Evening Reflection: As your day winds down, engage in a brief reflection. Consider what went well during your workday and what areas could benefit from improvement. Then, repeat your affirmations as a commitment to enhancing your skills and mindset. An example might be, "I am continuously learning and growing in my career."

By establishing this routine, you're making affirmations into the part of your daily life, reinforcing the belief in your capabilities and the positive direction of your career. As you consistently water this mental garden, the affirmations will take root in your subconscious, influencing your actions and decisions.

Using Affirmations in Goal Setting and Planning

Affirmations, when harmonized with well-defined goals, become an even more potent force in your career journey. Goals offer a clear destination, and affirmations are the compass that guides you there. It's not enough to wish for career success; you must chart a course and affirm your commitment to following it. Let's explore how to incorporate affirmations into your goal setting and planning processes.

Clarity in Goal Setting: Begin by establishing crystal-clear career goals. These should be Specific, Measurable, Achievable, Relevant, and Time-bound (SMART). For instance, "I will attain the position of Senior Project Manager within the next two years."

Affirmations as Anchors: Once your goals are defined, build affirmations around them. Affirmations act as anchors that tether you to your objectives. Align them with your SMART goals, such as "I am steadily progressing toward my goal of becoming a Senior Project Manager."

Repetition and Belief: The repetition of affirmations is key here. By consistently repeating your affirmations, you reinforce your belief in the attainability of your goals. It's not merely a mantra; it's a pact you make with yourself. Your affirmation becomes a reminder of your commitment to your career ambitions.

Visualizing Success: Alongside affirmations, practice visualization. Imagine yourself accomplishing your goals. Visualizing success is a dynamic way to make your affirmations more tangible. As you affirm your capability, pair it with a vivid mental image of your successful self in your desired role.

Affirmations and Planning: Integrating affirmations into your daily and weekly planning can keep you on track. When you're setting your tasks and priorities, incorporate your affirmations to maintain alignment with your career goals. If one of your affirmations is "I am a skilled negotiator," make sure that negotiation-related tasks find a place on your agenda.

In this way, affirmations serve as not only motivational mantras but also as pragmatic tools for success. They help mold your thought patterns, keeping you resolute on the path to your career ambitions. Whether you're strategizing for a major project or charting the course for your professional development, your affirmations will provide you with a steady undercurrent of confidence and determination.

Measuring the Impact of Affirmations on Your Career Success

Nurturing a garden takes time and patience. Similarly, the impact of affirmations on your career success doesn't manifest overnight. However, rest assured that affirmations are not mere words; they are the sparks that ignite the fire of transformation within you. To understand this transformation and measure the tangible impact of affirmations on your career, consider these approaches:

Journaling: Keeping a career-focused journal is a valuable practice. Write down your affirmations, your goals, and your daily reflections. Over time, you'll be able to look back and see how your mindset, attitudes, and career choices have evolved. You might notice an increased sense of confidence, better decision-making, and a clearer path toward your goals.

Progress Tracking: In your journal or a digital tracking tool, monitor your career progress over weeks, months, and years. Note your achievements, milestones reached, and the correlation between your affirmations and your accomplishments. If one of your affirmations was "I am a dynamic leader," track your journey to leadership roles or projects you've taken the lead on.

Feedback from Others: Seek feedback from colleagues, mentors, or supervisors. Inquire about your professional growth and development. Often, you'll find that the changes in your attitude and actions are reflected in the perceptions of those around you. This external feedback can be a powerful indicator of the transformation facilitated by your affirmations.

Self-awareness: Practice self-awareness to recognize shifts in your mindset. Are you more proactive, solution-oriented, or resilient in the face of challenges? Do you find it easier to overcome setbacks and stay focused on your goals? This internal awareness is a testament to the influence of affirmations.

Milestones Achieved: Consider the concrete milestones you've achieved in your career. These might include promotions, new certifications, successful projects, or expanded responsibilities. Trace the path from your initial affirmation to these milestones. You'll often find a direct connection between your positive self-belief and your career achievements.

Affirmations, when embraced with dedication and persistence, have the power to reshape the narrative of your career. They enable you to navigate challenges with unwavering resolve, take calculated risks, and grasp opportunities that may have seemed out of reach. As you reflect on your affirmations and their impact on your career success, you'll discover that they've transformed not only your professional journey but also the essence of your identity as a confident, capable, and resolute individual.

Chapter 3: Finding Clarity and Focus in Your Career

3.1: Mindful Self-Assessment

In our fast-paced, ever-evolving professional landscape, it's all too easy to get swept up in the current of our careers, carried along by deadlines, responsibilities, and the constant hum of the working world. We find ourselves navigating the maze of daily tasks, meetings, and projects, rarely pausing to reflect on the direction in which we're headed. It's in these moments of unceasing motion that we might question whether we're on the right path, whether our career is a true reflection of our desires and potential.

Mindfulness encourages us to slow down, to pause, and to turn our attention inward. It's a practice of presence and self-reflection, one that can help us evaluate our current career path with a clarity that is often obscured by the ceaseless bustle of the workplace.

Evaluating Your Current Career Path with Mindfulness

Mindfulness, in its essence, is the act of being fully aware of the present moment. It requires us to observe our thoughts, feelings, and surroundings without judgment. When we apply this state of awareness to our careers, we embark on a journey of self-discovery that can be equal parts enlightening and challenging.

To evaluate your current career path with mindfulness, start by setting aside a quiet moment. Find a space where you can be alone with your thoughts, free from distractions. As you sit in silence, take a deep breath and close your eyes. Allow your attention to shift inward.

Begin by considering your career, your role, and your daily activities. What does your work mean to you? How does it make you feel? As you explore these questions, notice any emotions that surface. Is there contentment, excitement, and a sense of fulfillment? Or is there restlessness, frustration, and a longing for something more?

The beauty of mindfulness is that it doesn't judge your feelings; it simply acknowledges them. As you evaluate your career path, you may find that some aspects bring you immense joy while others leave you feeling unsatisfied. This is the moment to embrace those feelings, to allow them to rise and share their wisdom.

The act of mindfulness encourages a non-judgmental curiosity about these feelings. If you find that your career path is primarily filled with frustration and discontent, don't berate yourself. Instead, inquire further. What is it about your current role that doesn't align with your desires or values? What specific tasks or responsibilities trigger these negative emotions?

Through this self-assessment, you gain a deeper understanding of your professional experience. Mindfulness is not about hastily jumping to conclusions or rash decisions; it's about listening to your inner wisdom and allowing it to inform your path forward.

Identifying Areas for Improvement and Growth

In our careers, as in life, there is always room for improvement and growth. Mindfulness can serve as the compass guiding us through the vast territory of self-improvement. With the insights you've gathered during your mindful self-assessment, you can pinpoint areas where growth and change are needed.

Start by looking at the aspects of your career that brought you joy and fulfillment during your assessment. What qualities or activities are responsible for these positive feelings? These are the areas where your strengths and passions align. Recognize them and embrace the opportunities they present for growth and expansion.

On the flip side, pay close attention to the aspects that triggered frustration or discontent. These are your potential areas for improvement. Are there skills you can develop, perspectives you can change, or tasks you can delegate to others? Mindfulness teaches us that our power for transformation begins with self-awareness. By acknowledging your career's pain points, you lay the groundwork for productive change.

Mindfulness also encourages us to approach growth and improvement with a compassionate heart. This means not only recognizing your areas for development but also acknowledging that growth is a gradual process. Just as you wouldn't expect a seed to become a towering tree overnight, you shouldn't expect instant transformation in your career. Give yourself permission to learn, adapt, and grow over time.

Setting Career Goals Based on Self-Assessment

The insights you've gained through mindfulness and self-assessment are the building blocks for setting clear and purposeful career goals. Rather than aiming for arbitrary destinations, you can now chart a course that aligns with your values, passions, and strengths.

Begin by defining your long-term career aspirations. Where do you see yourself in the future? What kind of work excites and fulfills you? These aspirations should be bold, compelling, and deeply rooted in your self-assessment. Let them be your guiding stars, pulling you forward with determination and focus.

Once you've established your long-term vision, break it down into smaller, achievable goals. These intermediate goals serve as the rungs of the ladder, allowing you to make steady progress toward your ultimate career destination. The key is to create goals that are specific, measurable, achievable, relevant, and time-bound (SMART). In doing so, you transform your vision into a clear and actionable plan.

For example, if your self-assessment revealed a desire to move into a leadership role, your SMART goals might include:

Within the next 12 months, complete a leadership development course.

Within 24 months, take on a leadership role in a project or team.

Within five years, secure a senior leadership position in your field.

In setting these goals, you're not only channeling your career aspirations but also honoring your present self. You're acknowledging where you are, recognizing where you want to be, and carving out the path to get there.

Remember that goals are not set in stone; they can evolve as you grow and learn more about yourself. Mindfulness allows you to adapt and refine your goals as your career journey unfolds.

Mindful self-assessment is the golden thread that adds depth and purpose to the professional life. It allows you to see your path with clarity and empowers you to set goals that resonate with your authentic self. Your self-assessment is a foundational step, and it's one that can be revisited and refined throughout your career.

3.2: Affirming Your Career Path

In our pursuit of career success and personal fulfillment, we often find ourselves navigating a complex and winding path. It's a journey marked by milestones and crossroads, triumphs and challenges, and, at times, a sense of doubt. This chapter is dedicated to one of the most powerful tools in your toolkit as you walk this path – the art of affirming your career choices.

Affirmations, when harnessed effectively, have the potential to be guiding lights, steering you toward the career of your dreams. They're not mere words; they're the compass that directs you toward the life you envision. So, let's delve into the depths of affirmations in the context of your career and explore how they can illuminate your way forward.

Aligning Affirmations with Your Career Aspirations

Picture this: You've set your sights on a specific career goal. You've visualized yourself in that high-rise office, speaking confidently in board meetings, and impacting your field. But the path to that corner office seems arduous, fraught with uncertainty, and perhaps even a few missteps. In these moments, affirmations become your unwavering companions.

Affirmations are more than mere wishful thinking. They are potent statements that align your thoughts, feelings, and actions with your career aspirations. They create a bridge between your current reality and your desired future. For example, you might affirm, "I am a successful marketing executive, and I confidently lead my team to achieve our goals."

This affirmation encapsulates your vision, your role, and your confidence, all in a single sentence. When you repeat it consistently, you're not only setting a clear intention for your career but also sending a signal to your subconscious mind. The subconscious is a powerful ally; it doesn't distinguish between your present reality and your desired one. It works diligently to bring your thoughts and beliefs into alignment with your career goals.

Affirmations allow you to bypass the negative self-talk that can often plague us during a job search or career transition. They provide a positive, proactive counter-narrative to self-doubt and fear. So, while navigating the path of your career, remember that affirmations are like the guiding stars that help you stay on course, especially during turbulent times.

Maintaining a Positive Outlook During the Job Search

The job search, or any phase of career transition, can be a rollercoaster of emotions. Rejections, unanswered applications, and uncertainty can cast shadows on your optimism. During these trying times, the role of affirmations becomes even more pivotal.

It's natural to experience setbacks during your career journey. The key lies in how you respond to them. Here, affirmations serve as your unwavering foundation, helping you maintain a positive outlook even when the world seems to conspire against you.

In these moments, affirmations act as your personal cheerleader, offering a constant stream of positivity and encouragement. For example, you might affirm, "I trust in the timing of my career path. Every experience, whether perceived as success or failure, serves my growth."

This affirmation, like a soothing balm, reminds you that every twist and turn in your career journey is a valuable lesson, a stepping stone to your destination. It urges you to believe in the process, to trust that the right opportunity will come your way when the time is right.

Affirmations during your job search encourage resilience and perseverance. They help you maintain a forward-focused mindset, reminding you to keep moving even when the road gets tough. They encourage you to see rejection not as a roadblock but as a redirection, a nudge from the universe to explore a different path.

So, when faced with the inevitable challenges of your career, remember that affirmations are your steadfast companions, whispering words of encouragement and reminding you of your intrinsic worth.

Staying Committed to Your Chosen Career Path
One of the most profound aspects of affirmations is their ability to reinforce your commitment to your chosen career path. The journey to success is filled with choices and crossroads, and there may be moments when you question your decisions.

Affirmations are your faithful affirmations of commitment. They serve as declarations of your unwavering dedication to your chosen path. For instance, you might affirm, "I am deeply committed to my career goals, and I persevere in the face of challenges."

This affirmation not only reaffirms your dedication but also prepares you mentally for the inevitable hurdles you'll encounter. It reminds you that commitment isn't just about success but about the willingness to face adversity head-on.

There will be days when you wonder if your chosen career path is the right one. In those moments, your affirmations act as the lighthouse that guides you through the storm. They help you recognize that doubt is part of the journey and that it doesn't negate your commitment. Instead, it's an invitation to revisit your goals, to adjust your course, and to continue forging ahead.

Affirmations transform commitment from a vague notion into a concrete reality. They remind you of the reasons you embarked on this journey in the first place and the profound impact you aspire to make in your chosen field.

Affirming your career path is a potent practice that infuses your career journey with clarity, positivity, and unwavering commitment. When aligned with your career aspirations, affirmations become the silent yet influential guides that keep you on track. In the face of job search challenges, they maintain your positivity and encourage resilience. And during moments of doubt, they solidify your commitment to your chosen path.

3.3: Mindful Decision-Making

In the daily hectic of our careers, every day unfolds with decisions—some significant, others less so. We constantly choose the paths that shape our professional journey, navigating through a maze of possibilities. But there are moments when the gravity of a decision dawns upon us. These are the pivotal crossroads in our careers, where choices possess the power to transform our trajectory.

Imagine this scenario: you're presented with a remarkable job opportunity. It's a role that seems tailor-made for your skills and aspirations, but it's located in a new city, far from your familiar surroundings. You face a decision that goes beyond the routine; it's a juncture that requires careful consideration. It's in moments like these that mindful decision-making becomes your beacon.

Using Mindfulness in Critical Career Decisions

Mindfulness is often associated with meditation and relaxation, but its applications are boundless. When it comes to critical career decisions, it's not about emptying your mind but rather about filling it with intention and awareness. The process of mindful decision-making starts with self-awareness.

Begin by acknowledging your thoughts and feelings. This means giving yourself permission to experience the emotions that swirl within you. Excitement, anxiety, doubt—they're all valid responses to major decisions. Take time to meditate on these feelings, without judgment. Allow them to rise, recognize them, and then, gently set them aside.

When we embark on the path of mindful decision-making, we peel back the layers of external expectations, the weight of societal norms, and the noise of the world. We listen, with clarity, to our inner voice—the voice that knows our values, desires, and authentic self. This voice is often shrouded in the clamor of modern life, but through mindfulness, it emerges, guiding us toward choices aligned with our true path.

Mindfulness grants you the mental space to consider the long-term implications of your decision. It encourages you to view your career not as a sequence of isolated choices but as a narrative that unfolds over time. A career is a journey, not a single step. Mindful decision-making helps us see how each choice is woven into the fabric of our professional story.

Weighing the Pros and Cons with a Clear Mind

Decision-making often involves the arduous process of weighing pros and cons. It's like holding a set of scales, with benefits on one side and drawbacks on the other. But in the flurry of data, how do we know which side carries more weight? This is where mindfulness becomes a trusted ally.

The clarity cultivated through mindfulness allows you to approach this balance with a serene perspective. Rather than frenetically tallying columns, you learn to discern the essence of each factor. Instead of seeking external validation or fearing judgment, you observe your internal responses to each aspect of the decision.

One of the key tenets of mindfulness is staying fully present in the moment. When you apply this principle to decision-making, it means considering the present but also how your choice will ripple into the future. Ask yourself questions such as: "How does this decision resonate with my long-term goals?" and "What kind of impact will this choice have on my overall well-being?"

Take a moment to breathe and focus on the considerations before you. With each breath, recognize that there is no universally correct answer. There's only the answer that's right for you, your aspirations, and your life. This perspective allows you to approach decision-making with greater equanimity.

Trusting Your Intuition and Affirming Your Choices
In the realm of critical decisions, your intuition—the quiet, persistent voice that whispers beneath the tumult of thoughts—can be a valuable guide. Mindfulness encourages you to tune in to this inner wisdom. Your intuition is the summation of your life's experiences, your values, and your authentic self.

Rather than seeking external validation or attempting to conform to societal expectations, take a moment to trust your intuition. When a choice aligns with your core values and aspirations, your intuition often responds with a sense of resonance. It feels right, not just rationally but deep within your being.

Affirm your choices by grounding them in your values and aspirations. Affirmations, often viewed as simple, positive statements, can play a profound role in decision-making. Repeating affirmations that align with your choice can provide a boost of confidence and a reminder of your intentions. Affirmations are like the North Star, guiding your path even when the night is darkest.

Let's revisit the scenario of the intriguing job opportunity in a new city. With mindful decision-making, you have explored your feelings, weighed the pros and cons, and listened to your intuition. You've discerned that this move aligns with your long-term career aspirations and personal growth. Your affirmations resonate with the choice, reinforcing your confidence.

As you make this significant career decision, you do so with a clarity that transcends the chaos of external expectations and societal pressures. You step forward with the assurance that your choice aligns with your authentic self, guided by the principles of mindfulness. Your journey unfolds, marked by choices that are not just professionally rewarding but deeply fulfilling on a personal level.

In the process of mindful decision-making, we discover that it's not about finding the perfect choice; it's about finding the choice that is perfect for us. In the intersection of mindfulness and career decisions, we find not only clarity and focus but also a profound connection with our true selves. Our careers become more than just a path; they become a reflection of our authentic selves and a journey of purpose.

Chapter 4: Leveraging Affirmations for Career Growth

4.1: Affirmations for Confidence and Self-Esteem

In your career journey, there exists a factors that often goes unnoticed and undervalued, yet it's the very factors that can strengthen the entire foundation of your professional life. This factors, my dear reader, is your confidence and self-esteem.

Career growth is not solely about skills, knowledge, or networking prowess. It's also deeply rooted in how you perceive yourself and the belief you hold in your abilities. Affirmations, those seemingly simple yet profoundly transformative statements, can serve as your beacon in the storm of self-doubt, your shield against imposter syndrome, and your guide to fostering unwavering self-esteem.

Building Confidence through Affirmations

Confidence is not a constant, unwavering entity; it's more like a tide that ebbs and flows. Even the most successful individuals have their moments of doubt and insecurity. But the beauty of affirmations is that they can act as anchors during those stormy times, grounding you and reminding you of your inherent worth.

Let's dive into the practical application of affirmations to build and bolster your confidence.

Affirmation: "I am capable and competent in my work."

This seemingly simple statement can have a profound impact. It's a reminder to yourself that you possess the skills, knowledge, and abilities required for your job. When you repeat this affirmation regularly, you start to believe it. You internalize your capabilities, and, in doing so, you exude a quiet, unshakable confidence in your professional endeavors.

Affirmations like this serve as a steady drumbeat of reassurance. They whisper in your ear, "You've got this," and gradually, that whisper grows louder until it drowns out the chorus of doubt.

Affirmation: "I learn and grow from every experience."

One of the key drivers of self-doubt is the fear of failure. We often chastise ourselves for our mistakes and setbacks, viewing them as evidence of our incompetence. But through the lens of affirmations, you can reframe these moments.

This affirmation encourages you to see every experience, whether positive or negative, as a stepping stone in your journey. It invites you to embrace the idea that even in failure, there are valuable lessons to be learned. When you adopt this perspective, setbacks become opportunities, and self-doubt transforms into self-assuredness.

Affirmation: "I trust my intuition and decision-making abilities."

Confidence in your decision-making abilities is a cornerstone of professional growth. It's what propels you forward, allowing you to make bold choices and seize opportunities. But self-doubt can paralyze even the most talented individuals, leaving them second-guessing every move.

This affirmation acts as a shield against such self-sabotage. It reminds you that your intuition is a powerful tool, honed through years of experience and learning. By repeating this affirmation, you reaffirm your trust in yourself, and over time, you'll find that you're more decisive, less hesitant, and your career path is no longer mired in uncertainty.

Overcoming Imposter Syndrome and Self-Doubt

Imposter syndrome is a silent, insidious assassin of self-confidence. It lurks in the shadows, whispering that you don't deserve your success, that you're a fraud who's about to be exposed. It's an affliction that plagues even the most accomplished individuals. But it can be defeated, and affirmations are powerful weapons in this battle.

Affirmation: "I am not an imposter; I am a competent professional."

This affirmation confronts the imposter syndrome head-on. It reminds you that your accomplishments are not accidents; they're the results of your hard work, talent, and dedication. Whenever that voice of self-doubt begins to murmur, this affirmation roars back with a defiant declaration of your competence.

Affirmation: "I deserve the opportunities that come my way."

Self-doubt often leads us to believe that we're not worthy of the promotions, the accolades, or the exciting new projects that come our way. This affirmation, however, tells a different story. It tells you that you are deserving, that your skills and dedication have earned you these opportunities, and you should seize them without hesitation.

Affirmation: "I am constantly growing and improving."

One of the most potent ways to silence the voice of self-doubt is through a relentless commitment to growth. This affirmation reminds you that your journey is one of evolution. It tells you that, rather than striving for perfection, you should strive for progress. When you embrace this affirmation, you recognize that your career path is a voyage of continuous improvement, and it's okay to make mistakes along the way.

Harnessing Self-Esteem for Career Advancement

Self-esteem, often intertwined with confidence, is the bedrock upon which your career is built. It's your perception of your own worth, and it influences every decision, interaction, and step you take in your professional life. Affirmations can be the craftsman's tools that mold and fortify this foundation.

Affirmation: "I am worthy of success and happiness."

Many of us carry deep-seated beliefs that success and happiness are reserved for others, not ourselves. This affirmation confronts that belief head-on. It's a declaration of your inherent worthiness, a statement that reminds you that success and happiness are not exclusive clubs but open invitations to those who truly believe in themselves.

Affirmation: "I embrace challenges as opportunities for growth."

In a world where challenges are often viewed as obstacles, this affirmation offers a different perspective. It tells you that challenges are not adversaries but allies in your quest for self-esteem and career advancement. By internalizing this affirmation, you welcome challenges with open arms, recognizing them as the crucibles that forge your strength and resilience.

Affirmation: "I am in control of my own destiny."

One of the most powerful affirmations for self-esteem is this simple declaration of agency. It reminds you that your career path is not dictated by external forces but guided by your choices and actions. It fosters a sense of ownership and empowerment, the belief that you are the author of your own professional story.

In the chapters of your career story, these affirmations are the ink that imbues your narrative with confidence and self-esteem. By weaving these affirmations into your daily life, you craft a tale of resilience, growth, and unshakable belief in your own worth. As you move forward in your journey, remember that the threads of confidence and self-esteem are yours to strengthen, and affirmations are your loom. With each repetition, you weave a stronger, more self-assured you into the peak of your career.

4.2: Affirmations for Networking and Relationship Building

In the ladder of career growth, one of the most harmonious and enriching steps is affirming the power of relationships. Whether you're just starting your career journey or well into the expedition, the connections you build can be the catalyst for your ascent. In this subchapter, we'll explore the transformative potential of affirmations in networking and relationship building, an often underestimated facet of career growth.

Strengthening Professional Relationships Through Affirmations

The foundation of any successful career is built upon the bedrock of professional relationships. Your colleagues, mentors, peers, and even superiors all play pivotal roles in your development. A well-considered affirmation can serve as a beacon, guiding you towards deeper, more meaningful interactions.

Affirmation 1: "I am a valued contributor to my professional network."

This simple yet potent affirmation reminds you of your worth within your professional circle. Repeating it helps reinforce your self-belief, making it easier to approach networking with the confidence that your insights and experiences are valuable.

Affirmation 2: "I am open to learning from others."

This affirmation serves as a humble reminder that you are not the sole fount of knowledge. Remaining receptive to the wisdom of those around you can lead to meaningful exchanges and, in turn, a stronger network. By making this a part of your daily affirmation ritual, you're embracing a growth mindset, which can be a magnet for people eager to share their expertise.

Affirmation 3: "I build bridges and dissolve barriers."

Networking isn't just about gathering contacts; it's about forming connections. This affirmation embodies the idea that your interactions are not just transactional but transformational. You bridge gaps, foster understanding, and make everyone feel welcomed. It is a commitment to be the link between ideas, people, and opportunities.

Leveraging Affirmations in Networking and Social Events

Networking events can be daunting, with the pressure to make a good impression and form connections that might impact your career. Affirmations can be your invisible companions, offering support during these high-stake gatherings.

Affirmation 4: "I am a magnet for like-minded professionals."

By repeating this affirmation, you set an intention that you'll naturally attract those who resonate with your goals and values. It's not about quantity but quality. When you believe that the right connections will gravitate towards you, you exude a magnetic confidence that makes networking events more enjoyable and productive.

Affirmation 5: "I communicate with ease and authenticity."

Social events can sometimes feel like a rehearsed play, but this affirmation helps you step into the role with authenticity. It's a reminder to be yourself and communicate naturally. By embracing this belief, you'll find it easier to strike up conversations, share insights, and form meaningful bonds.

Affirmation 6: "I am present and attentive in every interaction."

Networking events often come with a barrage of distractions. To combat this, this affirmation encourages you to be present in the moment, fully engaged in your conversations. When you're genuinely attentive, people notice. They feel respected and valued, deepening the connection.

Expanding Your Career Opportunities with Affirmations

Networking isn't just about immediate benefits; it's also about planting seeds that may bloom in the future. Affirmations can be instrumental in preparing the soil for these opportunities.

Affirmation 7: "I am open to unexpected opportunities."

This affirmation is a testament to your flexibility and adaptability. By embracing the unexpected, you remain open to career opportunities that you might not have initially considered. It's an affirmation that says you trust in your ability to make the most of any situation.

Affirmation 8: "I nurture professional relationships even in the absence of immediate gain."

This affirmation speaks to the heart of networking and relationship building. It's a reminder that not all interactions need to lead to immediate benefit. By nurturing relationships for their intrinsic value, you're sowing the seeds of goodwill that can later yield opportunities beyond your imagination.

Affirmation 9: "I am a source of support and empowerment for others."

The beauty of networking and relationship building is that it's a two-way street. This affirmation encourages you to be not just a receiver but a giver of support. By believing in your ability to empower others, you create a positive ripple effect, and in the world of networking, what goes around often comes around.

Affirmations in networking and relationship building are like silent companions, guiding you through the labyrinth of your career. They bolster your self-belief, keep you grounded, and help you navigate the ever-evolving landscape of professional connections. The affirmations offered here are not mere words but, when consistently integrated into your mindset, become a force that shapes your career journey.

Remember that relationships, like careers, are built step by step. Each interaction is a brushstroke on the canvas of your professional life. So, repeat your chosen affirmations daily, carry them with you to networking events, and let them become part of genuine connections that enrich your career. Through the power of these affirmations, you can make networking an authentic and gratifying aspect of your journey towards the peak of your career.

4.3: Affirmations for Resilience and Adaptability

In our professional lives, we often find ourselves navigating the turbulent waters of change and facing the daunting specter of adversity. It's during these moments that our ability to embrace change, exhibit resilience in the face of setbacks, and maintain unwavering focus becomes not only a testament to our character but a key determinant of our success in the labyrinth of our careers.

Developing Resilience in the Face of Setbacks

Life is an intricate move of highs and lows, successes and failures, and it's in these troughs and crests where we unearth our true potential. Setbacks, whether in the form of a project gone awry, a missed promotion, or a sudden shift in the industry's winds, are part and parcel of our professional journeys.

It's precisely in these moments that our capacity for resilience shines through. Resilience, that indomitable spirit that keeps us afloat when life's tempests threaten to engulf us, is an essential trait in our career toolkit. It's not just the ability to bounce back, but the audacity to bounce forward. And as we delve into the world of affirmations, it becomes apparent that they can be our steady companions on this resilient journey.

Affirmations, often dismissed as mere positive thinking, hold a profound place in helping us cultivate resilience. They act as gentle reminders of our strengths, our past triumphs, and the inner reservoirs of courage we possess. In the face of adversity, when doubt and self-criticism rear their heads, affirmations offer us a lifeline. They whisper to our inner selves, "You've faced challenges before, and you've triumphed. You are capable."

Consider the professional who, in the midst of a critical project's failure, affirms, "I am resilient and resourceful. I can learn from this setback and emerge stronger." This affirmation doesn't erase the disappointment but serves as a powerful anchor amid turbulent seas. It encourages the professional to reflect on past experiences, where resilience shone brightly, and emboldens them to apply the lessons learned.

Resilience, as nurtured by affirmations, isn't about denying the pain of setbacks but acknowledging it and responding with strength and determination. It's a recognition that life's setbacks are opportunities in disguise, and we have the power to transform them into stepping stones toward our career goals.

Using Affirmations to Embrace Change and Adaptability

The only constant in our professional lives is change. Industries evolve, job roles shift, and technology propels us into new frontiers. To flourish in such a dynamic environment, adaptability is not a virtue but a necessity. And affirmations can be our trusted companions on this journey of transformation.

Change often triggers discomfort, uncertainty, and resistance. We cling to the familiar because it's safe and known. But affirmations, grounded in positivity and self-belief, can be the catalysts that propel us from our comfort zones into the fertile grounds of adaptability.

When faced with a significant organizational change, such as a merger or restructuring, our minds often race with uncertainty. In these moments, an affirmation such as, "I embrace change with an open heart and a curious mind," can be transformative. It guides us away from the treacherous path of resistance and towards the embracing of the unknown.

Affirmations, by their nature, invite us to reflect on our inner narratives and belief systems. In the realm of adaptability, they challenge our fixed notions and encourage us to be open to new ideas, perspectives, and possibilities. It's a testament to the malleability of our minds and our capacity to embrace the ever-shifting landscape of our careers.

Consider the professional who's been tasked with implementing a new technological system, a task that seems overwhelmingly complex. An affirmation such as, "I am adaptable, and I can learn and grow in any situation," can be a beacon of hope. It enables a shift in perspective, turning a daunting challenge into an opportunity for personal and professional growth.

Staying Motivated and Focused During Challenges
Adversity can be draining, sapping our motivation and leaving us feeling adrift. It's during these challenging times that we must harness our inner resolve and maintain unwavering focus. Affirmations, as the silent champions of our minds, provide the fuel to keep our motivation and focus aflame.

The daily grind, the relentless deadlines, and the occasional setbacks can cause motivation to wane. In these moments, affirmations can be like gentle nudges, rekindling the spark within us. An affirmation such as, "I am driven, and every challenge fuels my determination," can be the matchstick that reignites our inner fire.

Maintaining focus in a world replete with distractions can be an arduous task. The ping of incoming emails, the siren call of social media, and the cacophony of daily life can pull us away from our goals. But affirmations, when wielded consciously, can serve as the unwavering rudders that keep us on course. They ground us in the present moment and remind us of our priorities.

Imagine the professional facing a daunting project that seems insurmountable. Amidst the chaos and stress, they turn to the affirmation, "I am focused and undistracted in pursuit of my goals." This affirmation acts as a steadfast reminder, helping them silence the noise and channel their energy into productive action.

Affirmations are not mere words but gateways to our inner reservoirs of strength and resilience. When harnessed effectively, they serve as compasses, guiding us through the ever-changing terrain of our careers. They are the whispered encouragements during moments of self-doubt, the catalysts for embracing change, and the fuel for unwavering focus. With each affirmation, we sculpt a mindset that's not only resilient but also adaptable, motivated, and resolute in the face of adversity and change.

The path to career growth, then, is not one devoid of challenges, but rather one where we acknowledge and embrace these challenges with open hearts and empowered minds. With the right affirmations, we can navigate the intricate journey of our careers with grace and tenacity, ultimately ascending to the peak of our professional aspirations.

4.4: Maintaining Well-being, Work-Life Balance, and Stress Management

In every career field, there exists a complex interplay between ambition, productivity, and well-being. Achieving career growth is a commendable goal, but it should not come at the expense of our mental and physical health. In our relentless pursuit of success, it's easy to disregard the signals that our bodies and minds send us, warning us of impending burnout. This subchapter delves into a topic of paramount importance: maintaining well-being, achieving work-life balance, and mastering the art of stress management.

Preventing Burnout and Managing Stress with Mindfulness

When it comes to career growth, it's all too common to fall into the abyss of relentless ambition. The pursuit of professional excellence often means working longer hours, taking on more responsibilities, and pushing our limits. We convince ourselves that this is the path to success, and while hard work is indeed a valuable component of achievement, it should not come at the cost of our mental and physical health.

Mindfulness offers a crucial respite in this whirlwind. It's not about meditating for hours on end or achieving a zen-like state amidst chaos. Rather, it's a moment-to-moment awareness of your thoughts, emotions, and surroundings. Mindfulness is the art of grounding yourself in the present and accepting it without judgment.

As you strive for career growth, it's essential to incorporate mindfulness into your daily routine. Begin with simple practices like mindful breathing. Taking just a few minutes each day to focus on your breath can clear your mind and reduce stress. When the demands of your job seem overwhelming, pause, and take a few deep breaths. This simple act can center you and offer a fresh perspective.

Mindfulness also encourages self-compassion, reminding you to treat yourself with kindness and understanding. In the high-stress world of career development, we're often our harshest critics. But being kind to yourself, acknowledging your limitations, and giving yourself the grace to fail at times can be profoundly liberating.

Furthermore, mindfulness allows you to recognize the early signs of burnout. It teaches you to listen to your body and mind, enabling you to detect stress and exhaustion before they become overwhelming. By understanding the early indicators of burnout, you can take proactive measures to prevent it.

Practical Methods for Balancing Career and Personal Life

A successful career does not exist in isolation. It is interwoven with the threads of your personal life. Balancing the demands of work with your personal life is an art, and like any art form, it requires practice and dedication. Neglecting your personal life in pursuit of professional success can lead to a hollow existence, where achievements in the workplace offer little solace.

Begin by setting boundaries. It's an often-undervalued skill, but one that is instrumental in achieving a balanced life. Boundaries help you define when work begins and ends, allowing you to protect your personal time. Clearly communicate your boundaries to your colleagues and superiors, ensuring that they respect your personal life.

Work smarter, not harder. One common mistake in career development is the belief that the more hours we put in, the more successful we will become. While dedication is critical, the quality of your work and the efficiency with which you complete tasks are equally vital. Delegate when possible, prioritize tasks, and make use of technology to streamline your workflow.

Remember that your personal life deserves the same attention as your career. Schedule personal activities and time with loved ones just as you would for work-related commitments. It's easy to lose sight of this balance, but it is in these moments of connection and relaxation that we find the resilience to navigate the challenges of our careers.

Strategies for Self-Care and Stress Reduction in a Demanding Work Environment

In the relentless pace of modern work environments, stress can feel like a constant companion. Deadlines, meetings, and demands from all directions can be overwhelming. It's in these moments that self-care and stress reduction become paramount.

One effective strategy is to identify your stressors. Take a moment to pinpoint the specific factors that trigger stress in your career. Is it an overwhelming workload, tight deadlines, or challenging colleagues? Understanding these stressors is the first step in managing them.

With your stressors in mind, consider time management techniques. Prioritize your tasks and tackle the most critical ones first. This not only boosts productivity but also alleviates the anxiety of impending deadlines. Consider breaking down larger tasks into smaller, more manageable steps. Completing these smaller steps can provide a sense of accomplishment and reduce stress.

Self-care practices should also become a part of your daily routine. Engage in activities that nourish your mind and body. Regular exercise, a balanced diet, and adequate sleep are fundamental for managing stress. In addition, consider mindfulness meditation as a practice to reduce stress. Just a few minutes of meditation each day can provide a renewed sense of clarity and focus.

Support systems are invaluable in navigating stress. Share your concerns and challenges with a trusted friend, family member, or mentor. Their perspective and guidance can offer new insights and alleviate the burden of stress.

The road to career growth is often paved with stress and challenges. But it's essential to remember that, in your life, your well-being and work-life balance are equally critical threads. Achieving professional success should enhance your life, not diminish it.

Chapter 5: Aligning Career Goals with Mindfulness and Affirmations

5.1: Setting Mindful Career Goals

Setting and achieving career goals is like charting a course for your professional journey. It's about having a clear vision, a well-constructed plan, and the mindfulness to navigate the twists and turns along the way. In this subchapter, we'll explore the art of setting mindful career goals.

Defining Clear and Achievable Career Goals

When it comes to your career, goals act as a compass, guiding you toward your desired destination. It's essential to define them with precision. Consider a vague goal, such as "I want to be successful." That statement, while noble, is akin to saying you want to visit a place without specifying the location.

Mindfulness prompts us to set clear, well-defined career goals. Begin by asking yourself the following questions: What does "success" mean to you? What specific achievements do you want to attain? Which milestones will mark your journey? The act of mindfulness encourages you to dig deep and articulate your aspirations in a concrete, tangible manner.

Consider this example: "Within the next three years, I aim to become a senior project manager with my current company, leading a team of 10 individuals and achieving a 15% increase in project success rates." This goal is specific, time-bound, and measurable. It paints a vivid picture of what success looks like for you.

Using Mindfulness to Prioritize and Plan for Success

Mindfulness is not just about setting goals; it's also about aligning your values and priorities with your ambitions. When you mindfully contemplate your career path, it becomes evident that every goal you set should resonate with your values and principles. For example, if you value work-life balance, setting a goal that demands excessive overtime might lead to conflict and dissatisfaction.

Mindfulness serves as a mirror, reflecting your inner values. Take time to explore what truly matters to you in your career. This might include factors like work-life balance, job satisfaction, financial stability, or personal growth. Once you understand your values, use them as a guiding force in setting your goals. This ensures that your objectives are in harmony with your core principles.

Furthermore, mindfulness can help you devise a plan that aligns with your career goals. It's not just about plotting a route; it's about being aware of every step you take. Mindfulness can keep you grounded as you navigate your career path, helping you remain present in each moment.

Mindfully planning for success involves breaking down your overarching career goals into smaller, manageable steps. Consider these steps as the building blocks that construct your career. This approach is akin to building a bridge, brick by brick, toward your career goals. As you lay each brick mindfully, you ensure that it's firmly in place before moving on to the next.

Monitoring and Adjusting Your Goals Mindfully

A mindful career is one that is not static but adaptable. It's important to recognize that your goals might evolve as you gain more experience, insights, and opportunities. Mindfulness allows you to monitor your progress regularly and adjust your goals accordingly.

Regularly reviewing your career goals enables you to stay on course. It's similar to using a compass during a journey: you periodically check it to ensure you're headed in the right direction. Likewise, your career goals need to be assessed and, if necessary, recalibrated.

Mindfulness offers a unique perspective on goal evaluation. It encourages you to reflect not only on whether you're achieving your goals but also on how these goals make you feel. Do your goals still align with your values and principles? Are they leading to fulfillment and satisfaction, or are they causing stress and burnout?

Being mindful of your emotions and experiences along the way is a powerful tool for gauging your career goals' effectiveness. If you find that a particular goal is causing more distress than growth, mindfulness grants you the awareness to reassess and modify that goal.

In this way, mindfulness isn't just about hitting targets; it's about creating a career journey that's fulfilling and aligned with your deepest aspirations.

5.2: Affirmations for Goal Achievement

In the landscape of our careers, it's not uncommon to find ourselves navigating through a maze of aspirations and ambitions. We set our sights on that next rung of the professional ladder, envisioning the growth and success that lie beyond. Yet, it's not the mere act of setting career goals that guarantees their realization; it's the unwavering commitment, the relentless persistence, and the belief in our capacity to reach those aspirations that truly set the wheels of achievement in motion.

In this subchapter, we delve into the power of affirmations as a remarkable tool for goal achievement. Affirmations, often underrated in their simplicity, have the potential to reinforce your commitment to your career goals. They serve as a reminder of your path, a source of motivation, and a touchstone for measuring progress. Here, we'll explore how to craft and employ goal-oriented affirmations effectively, offering a path to not only realizing your ambitions but also celebrating the journey.

Reinforcing Your Commitment to Career Goals with Affirmations

Your career goals aren't just waypoints on the map; they are reflections of your aspirations, your dreams, and the professional legacy you wish to build. However, in the hustle and bustle of everyday work, it's easy to get sidetracked, to lose sight of your purpose, or to be consumed by the demands of the moment.

Affirmations, in their essence, serve as a compass guiding you back to your true north, which is your career goals. They are concise, positive statements that remind you of what you aim to achieve. Consider an affirmation like, "I am steadily progressing toward my goal of becoming a marketing manager." It's a simple, present-tense declaration that echoes your commitment to your goal.

To make the most of affirmations for goal achievement, take time daily to recite them with sincerity. Engage in this practice with mindfulness, allowing your mind to fully absorb and internalize the affirmations. This process reinforces your commitment by instilling a sense of purpose and direction. It aligns your thoughts, emotions, and actions, thus enhancing your focus on the path to your career ambitions.

Measuring Progress and Celebrating Small Victories
One of the most powerful aspects of goal-oriented affirmations is their capacity to break down your long-term career goals into manageable milestones. While the end goal may seem distant, the journey is marked by countless smaller victories along the way. Affirmations provide a constant reminder that progress is not always about reaching the summit; it's about the steps taken, the growth achieved, and the lessons learned.

Consider an affirmation like, "I am making steady progress, one step at a time." This affirmation shifts your focus from the distant peak to the very step you're taking in the present. It encourages you to acknowledge and celebrate each step, regardless of its size.

Measuring progress in the context of career goals can be a challenging endeavor. Success isn't always quantifiable, and often it's the smaller, qualitative victories that matter most. Mindfulness, the practice of staying fully present in the moment, is essential here. It allows you to see the significance in the small victories, to be appreciative of the lessons learned in setbacks, and to understand that progress, no matter how incremental, is still progress.

Affirmations help you maintain this mindset. They remind you that every day, you're a little closer to your career objectives. And while the ultimate destination may be years away, today's progress is worth celebrating, for it's laying the foundation for your future success.

Staying Motivated and Persistent with Goal-Oriented Affirmations

In the pursuit of our career goals, motivation is the engine that keeps us moving forward. Yet, motivation is not a constant; it can ebb and flow like the tides. During those moments when motivation wanes, and the path ahead seems daunting, goal-oriented affirmations become a lifeline. They are the persistent, unwavering voice that whispers in your ear, "Keep going."

Your affirmations, carefully crafted and deeply internalized, serve as a wellspring of motivation. Consider an affirmation like, "I am resilient, and I never give up on my dreams." It's a declaration of your inner strength and determination. When the days get tough, and the journey feels long, this affirmation reminds you of your unwavering spirit.

Persistent, relentless action is the true key to achieving your career goals. It's not always about speed, but consistency. In those moments when you feel like you're pushing against the tide, it's the persistence fueled by your affirmations that propels you forward. It's a testament to your belief in yourself and your dreams.

However, persistence doesn't mean working yourself to the bone without respite. Mindfulness, coupled with affirmations, helps you find balance in your pursuit. It reminds you that it's okay to take breaks, to recalibrate, and to nurture your well-being. In fact, affirmations can include statements like, "I prioritize self-care to maintain my focus and determination." This emphasizes the importance of balance while staying committed to your goals.

Goal-oriented affirmations are not mere words; they are the catalysts for your career aspirations. They reinforce your commitment, guide you in measuring progress, and provide unwavering motivation. By internalizing these affirmations and pairing them with mindfulness, you build a steadfast foundation for the journey toward your career goals, celebrating each step along the way. This is the art of affirmation—simple, yet profoundly transformative.

5.3: Mindfulness, Affirmations, and Long-term Vision

In the hectic time of our daily lives, it's easy to get lost in the minutiae, focusing on short-term goals and immediate concerns. But true career success is a journey that extends beyond the next promotion or paycheck. It's about the enduring impact we make, the legacy we create, and the path we carve for ourselves in the long run. In this subchapter, we delve into the powerful combination of mindfulness and affirmations as tools to cultivate a long-term career vision, create affirmations that support our lifelong aspirations, and find the delicate balance between the present and a mindful eye on the future.

Cultivating a Long-Term Career Vision through Mindfulness

Mindfulness is often associated with being in the present moment, and rightly so. The ability to appreciate the current instant and experience it fully is a valuable skill. However, mindfulness is not just about the present; it extends to how we envision our future.

In the context of career, practicing mindfulness means being intentional about where you want to be in the long term. It's about gazing into the future with a clear, focused, and compassionate perspective. When you cultivate a long-term career vision through mindfulness, you create a mental space where your aspirations can grow and thrive.

Start by finding a quiet place, free from distractions, where you can sit comfortably. Close your eyes and take a few deep breaths, inhaling and exhaling slowly. As you relax, let your mind wander to the horizon of your career. Imagine where you want to be in five, ten, or even twenty years from now.

This mindful contemplation serves several purposes. It allows you to:

1. Clarify Your Goals: By envisioning your long-term career, you can clarify your goals and what truly matters to you. What legacy do you want to leave? What impact do you want to have on your industry or community?

2. Set Intention: Mindfulness helps you set an intention. It's not merely about setting a goal; it's about imbuing it with intention and purpose. Why do you want to achieve what you've envisioned?

3. Overcome Obstacles: When you visualize your long-term vision mindfully, you also acknowledge the potential challenges and obstacles along the way. This prepares you to face them with resilience and determination.

Creating Affirmations that Support Your Lifelong Aspirations
Affirmations are more than just positive phrases we repeat to ourselves. When aligned with our long-term career vision, they become powerful tools for manifestation. Here's how to create affirmations that support your lifelong aspirations:

1. Be Specific: Rather than using vague affirmations like "I am successful," make them specific to your long-term vision. For example, "I am a renowned expert in my field, making a lasting impact."

2. Use the Present Tense: Affirmations are most effective when you state them in the present tense, as if you've already achieved them. This activates your subconscious mind to work toward manifesting your goals.

3. Keep Them Positive: Frame your affirmations positively. Instead of saying, "I will not fail," say, "I am confident in my ability to overcome challenges."

4. Make Them Believable: Your affirmations should be believable and resonate with your values and self-concept. If they feel unattainable, your mind may reject them.

5. Repeat and Visualize: Consistently repeat your affirmations, and as you do, visualize them. Imagine the future where these affirmations have become your reality.

6. Stay Committed: Affirmations are a long-term practice. Even when faced with setbacks, continue to recite and believe in your affirmations.

Your affirmations will become your compass, leading you toward the career vision you've cultivated through mindfulness.

Balancing the Present with a Mindful Eye on the Future

Balancing the present moment with a mindful eye on the future can be challenging. In our relentless pursuit of long-term goals, we might neglect the joy and satisfaction that can be found in the here and now. But mindfulness teaches us that the present is not a hindrance to our future; it is the very foundation upon which our future is built.

Consider the delicate art of gardening. A gardener sows seeds, knowing that they will take time to sprout, grow, and bear fruit. Yet, the gardener doesn't obsess over the future fruit to the detriment of nurturing the present soil, watering the young plants, and shielding them from harm. In the same way, our career aspirations require us to cultivate the present moment with the same care and attention we invest in the future.

Balance begins with gratitude. Practice gratitude for your current position, your skills, and the opportunities you have today. Recognize that each moment is a building block for your long-term vision. Rather than rushing through tasks, engage with them mindfully. Quality work in the present lays the foundation for future success.

Mindfulness also reminds us to periodically pause and reassess. As you journey toward your long-term career vision, the path may need adjustments. Mindfulness encourages you to check in with yourself, ask if your goals remain aligned with your values, and make any necessary modifications to your plan.

Balancing the present with a mindful eye on the future is a continuous acts. It's about recognizing the beauty and potential in each moment, while never losing sight of the overarching dream. When you can find joy in both the journey and the destination, you're on the path to achieving your career aspirations.

The synergy of mindfulness and affirmations in the context of long-term career vision provides us with the clarity, intention, and balance needed to navigate our career journeys with purpose and fulfillment. By cultivating this harmonious relationship between the present and the future, we unlock the potential to achieve career success that resonates with our deepest aspirations and values. Remember, your career is not a destination; it's a lifelong journey. Embrace it mindfully, and let your affirmations light the way.

Chapter 6: Enhancing Communication Skills through Mindfulness and Practical Techniques

6.1: Mindful Communication and Active Listening

In our careers field, one constant remains: communication. It's the core that become foundation of our professional lives, connecting us with colleagues, superiors, clients, and partners. Effective communication is not merely the exchange of words; it's a dynamic process that influences relationships, decisions, and the trajectory of our careers. In this subchapter, we'll delve into the art of mindful communication and active listening, exploring how these skills can transform the way we interact in the workplace.

Combining Mindfulness with Active Listening Techniques

In our fast-paced world, we often find ourselves in conversations where we're physically present but mentally absent. The art of active listening is about reversing this trend. Active listening isn't just about hearing the words someone is saying; it's about truly understanding and empathizing with the speaker. When we introduce mindfulness into this equation, we transform our conversations into meaningful exchanges.

Mindfulness in communication is the practice of being fully present in the moment, free from distractions and preconceived judgments. To combine mindfulness with active listening, start by centering yourself in the conversation. Set aside your own thoughts, worries, and judgments, and direct your full attention to the person speaking.

Think of it as a dance—a dance of words and emotions. Pay close attention to the speaker's non-verbal cues: their tone, body language, and facial expressions. These cues often convey more than words alone can. By tuning in to these subtleties, you can respond not only to what's said but also to the unspoken feelings behind the words.

Practicing mindfulness in communication is like offering a hand to guide someone across a rocky stream. It says, "I'm here with you; I'm present in this moment." By being fully engaged, you open the door for deeper, more genuine conversations. You don't just hear the words; you understand the emotions, intentions, and nuances within them.

Improving Interpersonal Relationships through Mindful Communication

Mindful communication is the bridge to healthier and more meaningful interpersonal relationships. It's about treating every conversation as an opportunity to connect, learn, and grow. When we approach communication with mindfulness, we cultivate empathy, which is the cornerstone of understanding and building strong connections.

Empathy isn't a mere understanding of someone's emotions; it's the capacity to feel what they're feeling. In a mindful conversation, you not only listen actively but also immerse yourself in the other person's perspective. You don't rush to judgment or formulate responses while they're still speaking. Instead, you pause, take a breath, and truly grasp their point of view.

This level of understanding creates trust and fosters a sense of safety. When people feel heard and valued, they're more likely to open up, share their ideas, and collaborate effectively. In a professional setting, such connections are the bedrock of teamwork and leadership. They lead to productive discussions, innovative solutions, and harmonious working environments.

Imagine a workplace where every team member practices mindful communication. It's a place where colleagues appreciate each other's contributions, managers genuinely understand the concerns of their employees, and conflicts are resolved through meaningful dialogue rather than hostility. Mindful communication transforms workplaces into hubs of collaboration, mutual respect, and ultimately, career success.

Practicing Effective Communication Strategies for Career Success

Now, let's bring it full circle—how does mindfulness and active listening relate to career success? The connection is profound. In the professional realm, effective communication is an invaluable asset. It's the compass that guides you through the complex terrain of your career, helping you navigate everything from job interviews to team collaborations and leadership.

Think of your career as a journey, and effective communication as your map and compass. You may have the skills, education, and experience required for your job, but without the ability to express yourself clearly, understand others, and connect on a personal level, your success may remain elusive.

When you practice effective communication in your career, you exhibit a crucial skill: the ability to convey your thoughts, ideas, and aspirations with clarity and confidence. It's not about the grandiosity of your vocabulary; it's about the precision and power of your message. People often remember not what you said, but how you made them feel. Effective communication evokes feelings of trust, assurance, and respect.

Mindful communication ensures that you not only speak with purpose but also listen with intention. In job interviews, for instance, this can be the difference between just answering questions and truly connecting with the interviewer. You can respond to their inquiries with a profound understanding of their needs, and articulate how your skills and experiences align with their requirements.

Effective communication also extends to your relationships with colleagues and superiors. It's the tool you use to resolve conflicts, share innovative ideas, and contribute to team discussions. When you listen mindfully, you grasp the nuances of your colleagues' thoughts and feelings, which empowers you to collaborate more effectively. This, in turn, can lead to a more harmonious work environment and a higher likelihood of career advancement.

In leadership positions, the art of communication takes on an even greater role. It's about guiding and inspiring your team, setting a vision, and ensuring everyone is aligned with the goals. Mindful leadership communication is like the conductor of an orchestra, harmonizing the diverse talents of individuals into a symphony of success. It fosters trust and loyalty among team members, leading to increased productivity and achievement of organizational objectives.

Mindful communication and active listening are the cornerstone of your career success. They are the tools that allow you to build meaningful connections, foster trust, and communicate your ideas with impact. By incorporating mindfulness into your interactions, you're not only enhancing your personal relationships but also creating a path to professional accomplishment. It's a holistic approach to career growth that relies on the simple yet profound art of being present in your conversations and, in doing so, make stronger foundation on your career and life.

6.2: Conflict Resolution, Negotiation, and Mindfulness

Conflict. The very word often makes us squirm in our seats. It's not a topic we tend to lean into willingly. But it's precisely this avoidance of conflict that often leads to its escalation and an unproductive exchange of words, or worse, a deafening silence in which words left unspoken build invisible barriers between individuals. How do you navigate this treacherous terrain with mindfulness and practicality? Let's delve into the art of conflict resolution and negotiation, drawing on the profound power of mindfulness.

Applying Mindfulness in Conflict Resolution and Negotiation

It's tempting to approach conflict like a battlefield, where victory is defined by one party's triumph over the other. However, the mindful approach shifts this paradigm. Instead of seeing it as a battle, consider it a dance, one in which both parties must be attuned to the rhythm and flow of the conversation.

Mindfulness, in this context, means paying full attention to the person across from you, suspending judgments, and opening yourself up to truly understanding their perspective. This doesn't mean you have to agree with them, but it does mean acknowledging their viewpoint. It means that as they speak, you don't immediately construct your response in your head, but you actively listen.

Strategy 1: Active Listening

Listening actively is about more than hearing words; it's about grasping the emotions and intentions behind those words. It's not uncommon for people in conflict to speak past each other, their words crashing like waves against rocks. Through mindfulness, you can become the calm, receptive shore that listens and absorbs. In this state, you're not merely waiting for your turn to speak, but you're fully present, showing the other person that you value what they're saying.

Take a deep breath and allow them to express themselves. Don't interrupt, and don't immediately jump in with your perspective. When they pause, you might ask open-ended questions to encourage them to share more. For instance, you could say, "Tell me more about how you feel," or "What led you to this conclusion?"

Strategy 2: Mindfulness in Non-Verbal Communication

Communication isn't solely about words. Our non-verbal cues often speak louder than our words. Mindfulness extends to how you present yourself physically. Your body language should convey openness and receptivity. Maintain eye contact, adopt an open posture (uncross your arms), and nod occasionally to show you're engaged.

Also, consider your tone of voice. In conflict, it's common for voices to rise, and words to become heated. Mindful communication involves being aware of the tone you use and its potential impact on the conversation. A calm and even tone can help de-escalate tensions.

Strategy 3: Practicing Empathy in Conversations

Empathy is your most potent tool in conflict resolution and negotiation. Empathizing doesn't mean you agree with the other person, but it means you're willing to step into their shoes and see the world from their perspective.

To practice empathy mindfully, start by acknowledging their feelings. You might say, "I can see that this situation is really important to you, and it's causing you distress." This validates their emotions and fosters a connection. Remember, empathy doesn't equate to weakness; it's a powerful way to create understanding and trust.

Strategies for Resolving Disputes Mindfully
Mindful conflict resolution isn't about avoiding the conflict altogether; it's about approaching it with a clear and calm mind, focused on understanding and resolution. Here are practical strategies for resolving disputes mindfully:

Strategy 1: Take a Breath

It's astonishing how a deep breath can defuse a tense situation. When you feel the heat of conflict rising, take a moment to inhale slowly and exhale even more slowly. This simple act can help you regain composure and approach the conversation with a clearer mind.

Strategy 2: Identify Shared Goals

In many conflicts, it's possible to identify shared goals. Whether it's a disagreement between colleagues or a personal dispute, there's usually a common objective both parties want to achieve. Mindfulness allows you to step back and see the bigger picture. What are you both trying to accomplish, and can you find common ground? By acknowledging shared objectives, you can often find a more peaceful resolution.

Strategy 3: Focus on the Present Moment

One challenge in conflict is that it often dredges up past grievances or fears about the future. Mindfulness encourages you to stay anchored in the present moment. Instead of bringing up past mistakes or worrying about what might happen, concentrate on the issue at hand. What's the current problem, and how can you address it constructively?

Negotiating Win-Win Solutions Through Mindfulness

Negotiation is inherently about compromise. It's the art of finding a solution that benefits both parties. However, the process can be riddled with stress and the fear of giving up too much. Mindfulness can make negotiations more productive and less anxiety-inducing.

Strategy 1: Clarify Your Interests and Needs

Before entering a negotiation, take time to clarify your interests and needs. What are your non-negotiables, and where can you be flexible? Mindfulness allows you to recognize your core concerns and communicate them effectively.

Strategy 2: Understand the Other Party's Perspective

In a negotiation, it's equally important to understand the other party's interests and needs. This is where active listening and empathy come into play. By tuning in to their perspective, you can identify areas of potential compromise and collaboration.

Strategy 3: Stay Calm and Patient

Negotiations can be lengthy and emotionally charged. Mindfulness helps you stay patient and calm, even when faced with challenging moments. If things become heated, a moment of mindfulness can help you regain your equilibrium and continue with a clear mind.

Strategy 4: Explore Creative Solutions

Mindfulness can open your mind to creative solutions. Sometimes, the most innovative and beneficial agreements come from thinking outside the box. By staying present and receptive, you can explore new possibilities that satisfy both parties.

Conflict resolution and negotiation aren't about erasing conflict from our lives but about transforming it into a productive and growth-oriented conversation. When approached mindfully, conflicts become opportunities for understanding, collaboration, and win-win solutions.

6.3: Public Speaking and Presentation Mastery

Public speaking can be a daunting endeavor. Standing in front of an audience, all eyes and expectations fixated on you, can send shivers down anyone's spine. The familiar discomfort often associated with public speaking is, in fact, rooted in our innate fear of judgment and vulnerability. This subchapter is dedicated to unraveling the secrets of conquering public speaking anxiety, delivering captivating presentations, and acquiring the practical skills necessary for effective public speaking.

Overcoming Public Speaking Anxiety with Mindfulness

For many, the thought of public speaking triggers a potent cocktail of nervousness, anxiety, and self-doubt. The heart races, palms become clammy, and thoughts start to swirl like a tempestuous sea. This intense reaction is a byproduct of the human psyche's innate aversion to vulnerability. We fear judgment, ridicule, and the potential of failing in front of others. However, here's the secret to overcoming this anxiety: mindfulness.

Mindfulness, as we've discovered, is the art of being fully present in the moment. When it comes to public speaking, this means embracing the raw authenticity of the situation. Instead of trying to suppress your fear, accept it. Recognize that public speaking anxiety is a natural response to vulnerability. In this acceptance, you'll find empowerment.

Begin by grounding yourself in the present moment. Before taking the stage, find a quiet place to focus on your breath. Feel each inhale and exhale, letting it calm the turbulence within. This simple act of mindfulness centers you and allows you to acknowledge your anxiety without judgment. You're not weak for feeling this fear; you're human.

The practice of mindfulness in the context of public speaking is about recognizing the narrative playing in your mind – the stories of potential failure, humiliation, or inadequacy – and choosing to let them pass like clouds in the sky. By gently redirecting your attention to the present, you reclaim your power.

Delivering Powerful and Persuasive Presentations
Once the anxiety is tamed, the next challenge is to deliver a presentation that captivates and influences your audience. For this, we must understand that public speaking is not about performing but connecting.

The core of a powerful presentation is authenticity. Your message should resonate with your audience because it's a part of your truth. In other words, speak from your heart, not from a script or a mask of professionalism. The essence of persuasion lies in your ability to make your audience feel, not just understand. Storytelling is a powerful tool in this regard. We remember stories because they engage our emotions.

Take your audience on a journey. Share a personal experience, a relevant anecdote, or a powerful metaphor that relates to your topic. When they can connect with your narrative, they become emotionally invested in your message.

Practical Tips for Effective Public Speaking and Presentation Skills

The best way to become an effective public speaker is to practice and learn from experience. But here are some practical tips to start you on your journey:

1. Know Your Material: The more you understand your topic, the more confident you'll be. You should be able to discuss your subject matter without relying on your slides or notes.

2. Practice, Practice, Practice: Rehearse your presentation multiple times. This not only helps with content recall but also builds your confidence.

3. Engage Your Audience: Address your audience's needs and concerns. Ask questions, and encourage participation.

4. Use Visuals Sparingly: Visual aids are there to enhance, not replace, your words. Keep slides simple, and don't overcrowd them with text.

5. Voice Control: Work on your tone, pitch, and volume. A varied and expressive voice can keep your audience engaged.

6. Body Language: Pay attention to your gestures, posture, and eye contact. They should complement your message and make you appear confident.

7. Silence: Don't be afraid of silence. It's a powerful tool in public speaking. Use it to give your audience time to process information and for emphasis.

8. Manage Nervous Habits: Be aware of any nervous habits like pacing, fidgeting, or excessive filler words (e.g., "um" and "like"). Practicing mindfulness can help you become more conscious of and control these habits.

9. Feedback and Improvement: Seek feedback from peers or mentors. Constructive criticism is invaluable for growth. After each presentation, reflect on what went well and what could be improved.

10. Record Yourself: Use technology to record your practice sessions or actual presentations. Watching or listening to yourself can provide valuable insights into your performance.

11. Learn from Great Speakers: Watch and learn from accomplished public speakers. Observe their techniques,

how they engage the audience, and how they structure their speeches.

12. Visualize Success: Visualization is a powerful tool for reducing anxiety and enhancing confidence. Before your presentation, take a moment to visualize yourself delivering it with poise and impact.

The art of public speaking is not about being flawless; it's about being human. It's about sharing your knowledge, experiences, and ideas with the world in a way that resonates and inspires. By embracing vulnerability, practicing mindfulness, and continually honing your skills, you can become a masterful public speaker.

Chapter 7: Collaborative Success through Mindfulness and Proven Career Strategies

7.1: Team Building and Leadership

In the dynamic landscape of the modern workplace, achieving collaborative success is a fundamental goal. A successful team can achieve remarkable outcomes, and at the heart of every thriving team lies mindful leadership principles, practical strategies for fostering teamwork and cooperation, and proven leadership techniques for team success.

Mindful Leadership Principles for Team Building

The concept of mindfulness in leadership is like a gentle breeze that breathes life into the traditional, top-down management approach. In the realm of modern leadership, the qualities that truly set apart successful leaders are empathy, active listening, and the ability to lead with both their hearts and minds.

At its core, mindful leadership involves being present, open, and compassionate. It's about creating a space where every team member feels valued and heard. Mindful leaders recognize that their team is not just a collection of employees but a group of individuals with unique experiences, perspectives, and aspirations.

Leaders who practice mindful leadership cultivate a culture of trust and respect. They understand that trust is the foundation upon which teams are built. This trust is not merely a matter of professional competence; it's deeply personal. When team members trust their leaders, they are more likely to speak up, take risks, and contribute their best work.

One fundamental principle of mindful leadership is self-awareness. This is the cornerstone upon which emotional intelligence is built. Self-aware leaders understand their own strengths and weaknesses, and this self-awareness enables them to appreciate the strengths and weaknesses of their team members. They can play to individual strengths, allocate tasks thoughtfully, and provide support where it's most needed.

Practical Strategies for Fostering Teamwork and Cooperation

While mindful leadership lays the foundation, practical strategies bring the vision to life. Building a cohesive team that works collaboratively requires a thoughtful approach. It involves addressing the complex dynamics at play within a group of individuals with varying personalities, working styles, and communication preferences.

One practical strategy is setting clear expectations. When team members understand their roles and responsibilities, it reduces ambiguity and minimizes potential conflicts. Open communication channels are essential to achieving this clarity. Leaders who practice transparency and create a culture of open dialogue foster an environment where everyone is on the same page.

Another strategy for fostering teamwork and cooperation is acknowledging and appreciating the diversity within the team. Every team member brings a unique set of skills, experiences, and viewpoints. Effective leaders recognize the value of this diversity and encourage team members to share their perspectives. When team members feel heard and valued, they are more likely to contribute their best ideas.

Regular team-building activities and opportunities for collaboration outside of work tasks can be instrumental in breaking down barriers and building strong relationships. These activities create a sense of unity and camaraderie among team members, reinforcing the idea that they are not just co-workers but a team that supports and relies on each other.

Proven Leadership Techniques for Team Success

Leadership is not a one-size-fits-all endeavor. Different situations may call for various leadership techniques. Effective leaders are adaptable and can tailor their approach to fit the needs of the team and the goals of the organization.

One proven leadership technique is the "servant leadership" model. In this approach, the leader sees themselves as a servant to their team. They prioritize the needs of their team members, providing support, guidance, and resources to help the team succeed. This selfless approach fosters an environment of trust and mutual respect.

Another technique is transformational leadership. Transformational leaders inspire and motivate their team through a shared vision of the future. They encourage creativity, innovation, and a commitment to the organization's goals. Team members are inspired to exceed their own expectations and contribute to the team's overall success.

Leaders can also use the democratic leadership style. In this model, leaders encourage team members to participate in decision-making and problem-solving processes. This involvement gives team members a sense of ownership and responsibility, leading to a more motivated and engaged team.

Team building and leadership are vital components of collaborative success. Mindful leadership principles set the stage, promoting trust, self-awareness, and open communication. Practical strategies for fostering teamwork and cooperation create a collaborative environment where team members can thrive. Proven leadership techniques, such as servant leadership, transformational leadership, and democratic leadership, provide the tools leaders need to guide their teams towards success.

Ultimately, mindful leadership is not about micromanagement but about providing the support and guidance needed for a team to reach its full potential. As a leader, it's your responsibility to create a space where your team can shine, and these principles and strategies can help you achieve that vision of collaborative success.

7.2: Project Management and Productivity

In our modern professional landscape, project management stands as a pivotal component of organizational success. The ability to initiate, plan, execute, and close projects efficiently is a sought-after skill in the professional arena. However, in a world often characterized by tight deadlines, limited resources, and evolving priorities, the landscape of project management can be a challenging one to navigate. Yet, what if I told you that the secret to effective project management lies not just in spreadsheets and timelines, but also within the realm of mindfulness? That's right – mindfulness, that practice often associated with meditation and peaceful solitude, holds the key to enhanced project management and greater productivity.

Enhancing Project Management with Mindfulness

Let's begin by understanding the essence of mindfulness in the context of project management. Mindfulness, at its core, involves a deliberate and non-judgmental focus on the present moment. This practice encourages us to be fully engaged and aware of what we are doing, and this concept can be seamlessly applied to project management.

In the realm of project management, a mindful approach means being present during meetings, actively listening to team members, and acknowledging the subtleties within the project. It means creating a workspace that's conducive to deep concentration, removing distractions, and approaching each task with a heightened level of attention. This fundamental change in perspective can make a world of difference in the way projects are executed.

Mindfulness fosters an environment in which project managers and team members can better handle the ever-present challenges of project management. When we are mindful, we approach problems and setbacks with composure and clarity. We can adapt to change with greater ease and remain focused on the ultimate goals of the project. Mindfulness reminds us that even in the midst of chaos, there is the opportunity for serenity, and this serenity can be a powerful asset in effective project management.

Practical Project Planning and Execution Strategies
Mindfulness, while a valuable mindset to adopt, is only part of the equation. It's essential to complement this mindset with practical strategies that underpin the execution of a project. When we merge the serenity of mindfulness with strategic project management techniques, we can unleash the full potential of our teams and reach new heights of productivity.

First, let's delve into practical project planning. The initiation phase of any project lays the foundation for success. Being mindful during this phase means approaching it with an open mind and considering all possible options. Too often, project managers rush to conclusions without embracing the nuances of a situation. Instead, engage in brainstorming sessions that allow creativity to flow freely. Ensure that the goals are clearly defined, and the roles and responsibilities are understood by everyone involved.

Mindfulness also comes into play during the execution of the project. Here, it's essential to maintain a clear focus on the task at hand. Distractions are the enemies of productivity, and when they inevitably creep in, it's crucial to acknowledge them without judgment and then gently return to the task.

Practical strategies in project management often include setting clear objectives, defining key performance indicators, and tracking progress. Mindfulness can augment these strategies by encouraging reflection and assessment throughout the project's lifecycle. Mindful project managers periodically step back to evaluate the project's direction, the team's dynamics, and the overall well-being of the project.

Proven Approaches to Ensuring Project Success

Now, we come to the holy grail of project management – ensuring the project's success. Success in project management is not merely a matter of crossing the finish line but reaching it with all the objectives met and the team intact. To achieve this, we can draw from proven approaches that have stood the test of time.

Communication stands out as a foundational pillar in project management. Without clear and open communication, projects can quickly veer off course. This is where mindfulness demonstrates its value. When project managers and team members practice mindful communication, they listen to understand rather than to respond. They appreciate the nuances of each team member's perspective and create an environment in which ideas and concerns can be freely shared.

Mindful project managers also recognize the importance of adaptability. In the ever-evolving world of project management, changes and unexpected challenges are par for the course. A mindful approach enables project managers to pivot gracefully and make adjustments without the panic and chaos that often accompany changes in project direction.

The art of delegation is another critical element. Mindful delegation involves entrusting team members with tasks while being aware of their strengths and areas for development. It's about empowering individuals to take ownership of their work, fostering a sense of accountability and pride.

Project success is not solely defined by the outcome but also by the journey. A mindful project manager appreciates the value of recognizing and celebrating milestones along the way. This practice boosts team morale and motivation, making it easier for everyone to remain engaged and committed to the project's success.

By embracing the present moment, being fully aware, and actively participating in project management, we foster an environment in which productivity soars and projects flourish. In this combination of mindfulness and tried-and-true strategies, we discover the formula for collaborative success in the dynamic world of project management.

7.3: Effective Problem Solving and Decision-Making

In the world of careers and professional endeavors, challenges are not just inevitable but, in many ways, necessary. They are the crucibles through which we forge our skills, make decisions, and grow as individuals. Problem-solving and decision-making are at the heart of overcoming these challenges, and when enhanced by the practice of mindfulness, they become even more powerful tools for success.

Problem-solving Techniques Enhanced by Mindfulness

Problem-solving often starts with identifying a challenge or issue that requires resolution. But how do you approach it? In the corporate world, many turn to structured methodologies and analytical tools. While these have their place, we can't underestimate the profound impact that mindfulness can have on the problem-solving process.

Mindfulness, at its core, is about being fully present in the moment. It encourages us to be aware of our thoughts, emotions, and surroundings. When applied to problem-solving, it means being fully present with the problem at hand. It's about setting aside distractions, biases, and preconceived notions and engaging with the issue as it is, without judgment.

Imagine a scenario in which you're tasked with resolving a workplace conflict. Without mindfulness, you might jump straight into the problem, possibly influenced by your own emotions or opinions. Mindfulness, on the other hand, allows you to observe the situation without immediately forming judgments or reacting emotionally. This clarity and objectivity are essential for effective problem-solving.

The mindfulness-enhanced problem-solving process can be broken down into several steps:

Step 1: Awareness of the Problem

Mindfulness begins with awareness. Take a moment to fully understand the problem you're facing. What are the key elements, and what is at its core? This awareness is about seeing the problem as a whole, rather than as a collection of isolated issues.

Step 2: Defining the Problem

With mindfulness, you can define the problem more precisely. This clarity is essential because solving an ill-defined problem can lead to misdirected efforts. Mindfulness helps you strip away any assumptions and get to the root of the issue.

Step 3: Generating Solutions

Mindfulness encourages creative thinking. In this step, allow your mind to explore various solutions without judgment. Don't worry about whether they are feasible or practical at this stage. Just let your creativity flow.

Step 4: Evaluating Solutions

After generating a range of potential solutions, use mindfulness to assess each one impartially. Mindfulness prevents you from becoming overly attached to a particular solution, allowing you to evaluate each on its merits.

Step 5: Making a Decision

Mindfulness can provide the clarity needed to make a decision. Instead of second-guessing yourself, you can trust that you've approached the problem rationally and with an open mind.

Decision-Making Processes and Strategies

Effective decision-making is a cornerstone of success in both our personal and professional lives. When making choices, especially significant ones, we often feel the weight of responsibility and the fear of making a wrong decision. Mindfulness can be a guiding light in this process.

Imagine you're at a career crossroads, and you have two equally compelling job offers. The decision-making process might feel daunting. However, when you apply mindfulness, you bring a new level of awareness to your decision.

Step 1: Clarify Your Values

Mindfulness begins with understanding your values and what truly matters to you. Before making any decision, it's essential to reflect on what aligns with your core principles and long-term goals.

Step 2: Gather Information

Once you've clarified your values, it's time to gather information about your options. Research the job offers, consider the company culture, the potential for growth, and how each aligns with your values.

Step 3: Mindful Reflection

This is the stage where mindfulness shines. Take time to reflect on your options without external distractions. Meditation can be a valuable tool here. By focusing your attention on your breath and staying present, you can gain clarity about your feelings and intuition regarding each option.

Step 4: Trust Your Intuition

Mindfulness allows you to connect with your inner wisdom. If, after reflection, one option feels more aligned with your values and intuition, it's a sign to trust your judgment.

Step 5: Accept Imperfection

Mindful decision-making acknowledges that no decision is perfect. Understand that any choice involves some level of uncertainty, and that's okay. The key is to make the best decision you can with the information available.

Resolving Challenges and Disputes Through Proven Methods

In our professional lives, we often find ourselves in situations where disputes or challenges arise. These can range from conflicts with colleagues to disagreements over project direction. When such issues surface, mindfulness can be a guiding principle in resolving them.

Step 1: Mindful Assessment

Start by mindfully assessing the situation. What are the facts? What are your emotions telling you? Pay attention to your thoughts and reactions without judgment.

Step 2: Empathetic Listening

One of the most powerful ways to resolve disputes is through empathetic listening. Mindfully listen to the other party's perspective without immediately responding. Truly understand their viewpoint and emotions.

Step 3: Mindful Communication

When it's your turn to speak, do so mindfully. Choose your words carefully, being aware of the impact they may have. Stay calm and focused on the desired resolution.

Step 4: Collaborative Problem-Solving

Mindfulness encourages collaboration and a focus on solutions. Together with the other party, explore potential solutions, seeking common ground and compromise.

Step 5: Mindful Conflict Resolution

Finally, reach a resolution mindfully. This means acknowledging the emotions that may have arisen during the process and finding a solution that satisfies both parties.

Mindfulness, when applied to problem-solving and decision-making, becomes a powerful ally in the professional world. It promotes clarity, creativity, and emotional intelligence, all of which are crucial for success in our careers. By practicing mindfulness in these areas, we not only navigate challenges with greater ease but also grow as individuals, enhancing our professional journey.

To achieve success in our careers, it is not enough to merely coast along, handling challenges as they come. We must be proactive and mindful in our problem-solving, decision-making, and conflict resolution. These skills, when combined with the principles of mindfulness, pave the way for a fulfilling and successful career.

Chapter 8: Lifelong Learning, Skill Development, and Practical Career Growth

8.1: Mindful Continuous Learning and Skill Enhancement

In the field of our careers, one thing remains constant – the need for continuous learning and skill development. The modern workplace is a dynamic ecosystem, a realm where stagnation is often the antithesis of growth. To remain relevant and reach the zenith of your career, you must embrace a growth mindset through mindfulness, implement strategies for continuous skill development, and leverage proven methods for mastering new skills and knowledge.

Embracing a Growth Mindset through Mindfulness

The concept of a growth mindset is not novel, but it's one that requires deliberate cultivation. Carol Dweck, a renowned psychologist, introduced this idea. She proposed that individuals can fall into two categories: those with a fixed mindset and those with a growth mindset. A fixed mindset believes that abilities and intelligence are static traits, while a growth mindset sees them as qualities that can be developed through dedication and hard work.

But how does mindfulness fit into this narrative? Mindfulness serves as the bridge that connects your desire for growth with the practice of nurturing a growth mindset. It enables you to remain present, fully engaged with the learning process, and open to embracing challenges as opportunities for personal and professional development.

Mindfulness encourages you to observe your thoughts and emotions without judgment. This means you can recognize self-limiting beliefs or negative self-talk that might otherwise hinder your growth. As you observe these patterns, you have the power to challenge and replace them with affirmations of your potential and capacity to learn.

Picture a scenario where you're tasked with learning a new programming language for your job. Your initial thoughts may drift towards doubts - "I'm not good at coding," "This will be too hard," "I'm not smart enough." In a mindful state, you can observe these thoughts as they surface, acknowledge them without judgment, and then counteract them with affirmations that foster a growth mindset: "I can learn anything I set my mind to," "Challenges are opportunities for growth," "With dedication, I can master this."

In this way, mindfulness equips you to embrace new skills and knowledge as exciting challenges rather than daunting obstacles. It encourages you to view the learning process as a journey, not a destination. With every step forward, every new skill acquired, and every bit of knowledge assimilated, you're nurturing a growth mindset that propels you towards the peak of your career.

Strategies for Continuous Skill Development
Continuous skill development isn't a luxury in the modern workplace; it's a necessity. To ensure you're not left behind as the career landscape evolves, you must actively seek opportunities to enhance your skills.

Consider this as a deliberate strategy rather than a reaction to external pressures. One of the most effective strategies for continuous skill development is setting clear and achievable learning goals. These goals should align with your career aspirations and be specific, measurable, and time-bound. For example, if you aspire to become a more effective project manager, your goal could be, "I will complete a project management certification within the next six months."

Once you've defined your learning goals, the next step is to design a learning plan. This plan should encompass various aspects such as the resources you need, the time you can dedicate to learning, and the learning methods that suit your preferences. If we continue with the project management example, your learning plan might include enrolling in an online certification program, dedicating a specific number of hours each week to study, and setting aside time for practice and application of your newfound knowledge.

An essential component of skill development is the application of what you've learned. This practical component bridges the gap between theory and real-world proficiency. It's here that mindfulness takes a prominent role. As you learn new skills, mindfulness encourages you to remain present and fully engaged in your endeavors. It's not just about absorbing knowledge; it's about understanding its practical implications and how it can be harnessed to solve real-world problems.

In the process, you may face challenges and setbacks, but a growth mindset - nurtured through mindfulness - will enable you to view these as stepping stones to mastery, not stumbling blocks. Embrace these challenges, learn from your mistakes, and refine your skills continuously.

Proven Methods for Mastering New Skills and Knowledge

Learning new skills and knowledge is one part of the equation, but mastering them is where the true value lies. Mastery implies not only understanding a subject deeply but being able to apply that understanding effectively.

One proven method for mastering new skills is deliberate practice. Coined by psychologist K. Anders Ericsson, deliberate practice involves a systematic approach to skill improvement. It's not just about repetition; it's about purposeful and focused practice that pushes the boundaries of your current abilities.

Deliberate practice is a systematic and highly focused method of skill improvement that transcends mere repetition and takes your abilities to new heights.

Focused and Purposeful Practice:

Deliberate practice is characterized by its purposeful nature. It involves practicing with a specific goal in mind and a conscious effort to improve a particular aspect of your skill. In contrast to casual or mindless repetition, deliberate practice is an active and engaged process.

Targeted Improvement:

When engaging in deliberate practice, you identify a specific area or skill you want to enhance. This skill could be a component of a larger skill set or a sub-skill that contributes to your overall proficiency. For instance, if you're a pianist looking to improve your finger dexterity, you would target exercises and techniques specifically designed to enhance finger agility.

Feedback and Assessment:

A crucial component of deliberate practice is the ongoing feedback loop. You regularly assess your performance and receive feedback, often from a coach, mentor, or through self-assessment. This feedback helps you identify areas for improvement and adjust your practice accordingly. It highlights your weaknesses and guides your efforts towards overcoming them.

Challenging Your Limits:

Deliberate practice requires pushing the boundaries of your current abilities. It involves engaging in tasks that are slightly beyond your comfort zone. This deliberate stretching of your skills keeps you in a state of "optimal discomfort," where you're challenged but not overwhelmed. By working at the edge of your current competence, you foster growth.

Sustained Effort:

Deliberate practice is an ongoing and often demanding process. It requires sustained effort and dedicated practice over an extended period. This kind of commitment distinguishes it from occasional or sporadic efforts to improve a skill.

Mental Engagement:

Beyond physical practice, deliberate practice also involves mental rehearsal and visualization. It's about developing a deep understanding of the skill you're trying to master. This mental engagement complements the physical practice and contributes to a more profound level of mastery.

As you engage in deliberate practice, mindfulness is your steadfast companion. It encourages you to be fully immersed in the practice, attentively observing your performance, and actively seeking areas for improvement. It also helps you manage frustration and maintain a growth mindset as you encounter difficulties. Your path to the peak of your career is paved with these acquired skills and the mindset to match.

8.2: Affirmations for Personal Growth and Career Development

In the pursuit of career excellence, it's not uncommon to focus solely on the external factors—the promotions, the paychecks, the corner office with a view. We often forget that our careers are intrinsically tied to our personal growth. The path to professional success is intertwined with our development as individuals. In this subchapter, we're going to explore how affirmations can serve as your guiding star, illuminating the path to personal growth and career development.

Using Affirmations to Set and Achieve Personal Development Goals

Imagine standing at the base of a mountain. Your career is that towering peak, and you're just starting the ascent. You look up, and the path seems steep and daunting. It's easy to feel overwhelmed, and doubt may start to creep in. Can you really make it to the top?

This is where affirmations come into play. They are like the trail markers guiding you on your journey. Affirmations are positive, present-tense statements that reinforce your beliefs about yourself and your goals. They are not merely empty words; they are your declarations of intent.

The first step is to set clear and actionable personal development goals. This isn't about vague dreams of success; it's about the concrete steps you can take. An affirmation, in this context, is your commitment to these goals. For instance, if your goal is to improve your leadership skills, your affirmation might be: "I am a confident and effective leader, and I am continuously growing in my abilities."

Notice the present tense. Affirmations are not about the future; they are about the now. They shape your mindset to believe that you are already on the path to success. By repeating your affirmation daily, you engrain this belief into your subconscious.

Affirmations are like the compass that keeps you on course. When the path gets tough, they remind you of your direction, and they help you stay true to your commitment. Repeating these affirmations isn't a hollow exercise; it's a daily reminder of your potential and your path forward.

Measuring Progress and Celebrating Achievements with Affirmations

As you continue your journey, it's essential to keep track of your progress. Much like a hiker measures the distance covered and the altitude gained, you, too, should monitor your advancements. Affirmations are not just for setting goals; they also serve as a tool for celebrating your achievements along the way.

Incorporate your successes into your affirmations. For instance, if you've successfully led a project and achieved your desired outcomes, your affirmation could be: "I am a skilled leader who consistently delivers results and positively impacts my team." This isn't boasting; it's an acknowledgment of your growth and success.

Progress often unfolds in small steps. It's easy to overlook these incremental achievements in the quest for grand milestones. However, by using affirmations to recognize and celebrate these small victories, you build a positive feedback loop that fuels your motivation and self-belief.

Transforming Self-Limiting Beliefs and Achieving Personal Growth with Practical Strategies

One of the most powerful aspects of affirmations is their ability to help you confront and transform self-limiting beliefs. These are the internal barriers we often place in our own way. "I'm not smart enough," "I don't have the experience," "I'm not a good leader." Sound familiar?

Affirmations serve as the sledgehammer to break down these walls. When you catch yourself thinking in self-limiting terms, replace those thoughts with affirmations that contradict them. If you find yourself doubting your abilities, affirm, "I am constantly learning and growing, and I am fully capable of achieving my goals."

By using affirmations in this way, you begin to rewire your thought patterns. You shift from self-doubt to self-belief. You change your inner narrative from "I can't" to "I can."

Now, let's be clear—affirmations alone won't magically erase your self-limiting beliefs. They are a tool, not a magic spell. It takes dedication, practice, and consistency. But over time, you'll begin to notice a shift in your thinking. You'll find that those self-limiting beliefs, once so powerful, begin to lose their grip on your mind.

Think of affirmations as your mental workout routine. Just as a physical workout builds your muscles over time, affirmations build your mental strength. You persistently train your mind to focus on your capabilities rather than your limitations.

Affirmations, when used strategically, can be a catalyst for personal growth. They serve as your constant companions on your career journey. They remind you of your goals, celebrate your achievements, and challenge the doubts that threaten your progress. They are your allies, pushing you toward the peak of your potential.

To illustrate this transformative power of affirmations, let's consider a hypothetical situation: Annie, a marketing professional, aspires to move into a leadership role within her organization. However, she struggles with self-doubt and a fear of inadequacy. Here's how Annie can use affirmations to set and achieve her personal development goals:

Setting Affirmations for Personal Growth:

- Affirmation 1: "I am a confident and capable leader."

- Affirmation 2: "I continuously develop my leadership skills."

- Affirmation 3: "I am deserving of a leadership role."

Measuring Progress and Celebrating Achievements:

- After successfully leading a project, Annie updates her affirmations:

- Affirmation 1: "I am a confident and capable leader who has a track record of success."

- Affirmation 2: "I consistently develop my leadership skills and see the positive impact on my team."

- Affirmation 3: "I am deserving of a leadership role and have demonstrated my readiness."

Transforming Self-Limiting Beliefs:

- When self-doubt creeps in, Annie reframes her thoughts with affirmations:

- Doubt: "I don't have enough experience for a leadership role."

- Affirmation Response: "I continuously develop my leadership skills and have successfully led projects. I am fully capable of taking on a leadership role."

Annie's affirmations serve as a daily reminder of her growth and potential.

 They help her confront self-limiting beliefs and celebrate her achievements, ultimately propelling her toward her goal of a leadership position.

The power of affirmations lies in their consistency and the conscious effort to replace self-limiting beliefs with self-empowering thoughts. When used as a tool for personal growth, affirmations can be a driving force in your journey to career excellence. Remember, your career ascent is not just about reaching the peak but also about the profound transformation that occurs along the way.

8.3: Navigating Career Transitions with Mindfulness and Proven Approaches

In the ever-evolving landscape of today's professional world, the concept of a linear, uninterrupted career path is rapidly becoming a relic of the past. Gone are the days when we entered a job right out of college and retired from it decades later. The modern career journey is more of a dynamic mosaic, an intricate weaving of different experiences, skills, and roles. It's the understanding that career transitions, whether voluntary or involuntary, are not interruptions but rather pivotal points in the narrative of our professional lives.

Transitioning from one career to another can be both exhilarating and daunting. It might be prompted by a deep yearning for change, a reevaluation of your passions and goals, or external forces that necessitate adaptation. Such transitions can, understandably, stir up a whirlwind of emotions and questions. It's in these moments of uncertainty that mindfulness and a strategic blend of proven approaches come into play.

Applying Mindfulness and Affirmations During Career Transitions

The first step in a successful career transition is understanding where you are coming from and where you wish to go. It involves a level of self-reflection that is often neglected in the hustle of our daily professional lives. Mindfulness, the art of being fully present and self-aware, is an invaluable tool in this process.

Mindfulness, in the context of career transitions, can mean grounding yourself in the present moment and acknowledging the emotions that come with change. It's about taking time to reflect on your current role, understanding your motivations for seeking a transition, and addressing any fears or doubts that may arise. When you mindfully approach your career transition, you're better equipped to make thoughtful decisions.

One mindfulness technique that can be particularly effective during career transitions is journaling. Taking a few moments each day to jot down your thoughts, feelings, and goals can provide clarity. It allows you to track your progress and identify patterns in your thinking. Affirmations, those powerful, positive statements that help reframe your beliefs, can work in tandem with mindfulness. They serve as reminders that you are capable, worthy, and equipped to take on new challenges.

Strategies for Successful Career Changes

A successful career change involves more than merely desiring it; it demands strategic planning and thoughtful execution. It begins with meticulous research and analysis. You must investigate your intended field or industry thoroughly. What are the skills and qualifications required? What's the job market like? How can your current skills and experiences be leveraged in the new context?

One crucial strategy in career transitions is to bridge the skill gap. This means actively acquiring the abilities and knowledge that are needed in your target career. Skill development can take various forms, from enrolling in courses or workshops to self-study and mentorship. This strategy is where the proven approaches come into play. You can draw upon the experiences of those who've successfully navigated similar transitions. Seek out mentors or professionals in your desired field for guidance. Their insights can be invaluable in helping you identify the skills that truly matter and offering practical advice on gaining them.

Networking, often considered the lifeblood of career progression, takes on an even more crucial role during transitions. It's not just about who you know but how well you know them and how they can support your journey. Mindfulness can be applied here too. When engaging in networking, be fully present in your interactions. Listen attentively and offer genuine value to your connections. Affirmations can provide you with the confidence to approach potential mentors and colleagues and articulate your goals clearly.

Achieving Success in New Career Endeavors with Practical Adaptation Methods

The ultimate measure of a career transition's success is your ability to excel in your new role. This phase requires the practical adaptation methods that make your hard-earned skillset applicable to your fresh surroundings. This is where the collections of your previous experiences, skills, and personal growth becomes foundation of your new career.

But adaptation is more than a mere grafting of past experiences onto new soil. It necessitates a level of humility and openness that allows you to learn and grow in unfamiliar territory. It's about recognizing that, no matter how seasoned you may be in your previous career, you're now a novice in your new field.

Mindfulness guides you in embracing this transition with patience and an open heart. It teaches you to approach each day as a new opportunity for learning and growth. When we practice mindfulness, we create the space to listen to others, to absorb their knowledge and experiences, and to adapt with grace. This can be an invigorating and liberating experience. It's the realization that your journey is not about clinging to a static identity but about evolving and adapting.

Affirmations can help anchor you in your new role. They are the daily reminders of your potential, your capacity to learn, and your commitment to growth. In the face of challenges, affirmations can be the beacon that reminds you that you're on the right path. They're not just words; they're beliefs that you cultivate daily.

While navigating career transitions with mindfulness and proven approaches can be incredibly rewarding, it's essential to acknowledge that it's not a linear journey. It's a series of steps, stumbles, and strides. Career transitions can be accompanied by setbacks, doubts, and even moments of imposter syndrome. But, as we mindfully engage in these transitions, we recognize that setbacks are stepping stones and doubts are opportunities for growth.

In the field of our professional lives, career transitions are the factors that create new patterns and designs. Embracing them with mindfulness and practical strategies is like dive in the colors of possibility and transformation. It's a reminder that our careers are not static landscapes but evolving masterpieces, waiting to be painted with the strokes of our mindful adaptation and the brushstrokes of our affirmations.

In the end, a career transition is not just about changing jobs or industries; it's a profound transformation of self. It's a journey that tests your resilience and determination, and, with the right mindset, it can be the most rewarding chapter in your professional story. So, as you embark on your own career transition, remember that you possess the power of mindfulness and the wisdom of proven approaches.

Chapter 9: Mindful Leadership and Practical Leadership Strategies

9.1: Leading with Mindfulness and Authenticity

In the world of leadership, authenticity is the foundational stone on which trust, credibility, and team motivation are built. It's the quality that elevates a good leader to a great one, and it's the glue that binds the intricate elements of mindful leadership together.

Integrating Mindfulness into Authentic Leadership

Before we delve deeper into authenticity, let's talk about mindfulness – a concept often misinterpreted as a mere buzzword or a fleeting trend. But it's more profound than that. Mindfulness, in a leadership context, means being fully present, not just physically, but mentally and emotionally, in every moment. It's about showing up as a leader in the truest sense.

Think of mindfulness as the compass that guides authentic leadership. It's about self-awareness, recognizing your values, and understanding your emotional responses. When you're mindful, you can't help but be authentic because you're in tune with your own thoughts, feelings, and intentions.

An authentic leader doesn't try to be someone they're not. They understand their strengths and vulnerabilities and embrace them. When you practice mindfulness, it helps you be aware of your reactions and navigate through the complexities of leadership with poise and grace. It's about responding rather than reacting, a vital distinction for a leader.

Building Trust and Credibility through Practical Leadership Strategies

Authentic leadership hinges on trust and credibility. When you're genuine and honest, people instinctively trust you. But trust isn't built overnight; it's cultivated through consistency and reliability. Authentic leaders walk the talk. They're not just saying the right things; they're doing them.

Let's delve into some practical strategies for building trust and credibility:

1. Be Transparent: In a world where transparency is often a scarce resource, being open about your intentions, decisions, and the reasoning behind them is like a breath of fresh air. Authentic leaders don't hide behind a veil of secrecy. They share the 'why' and the 'how' of their actions.

2. Listen Actively: Communication isn't just about talking; it's equally about listening. Authentic leaders listen actively to their team members, clients, and stakeholders. They value others' perspectives and incorporate valuable input into their decisions.

3. Keep Promises: Nothing erodes trust faster than unfulfilled promises. An authentic leader makes commitments carefully and ensures they follow through on them. When they say they'll do something, they do it. This consistency builds trust over time.

4. Admit Mistakes: Authentic leaders aren't infallible; they make mistakes like everyone else. However, what sets them apart is their willingness to admit when they're wrong. They take responsibility for their errors and use them as opportunities for growth.

5. Show Empathy: Understanding and acknowledging others' feelings and experiences is a crucial element of authentic leadership. Empathy creates bonds and demonstrates that you genuinely care about your team.

Proven Approaches to Inspiring and Motivating Teams

Motivating and inspiring a team isn't about grand gestures or motivational speeches. It's about understanding what drives each team member and aligning their motivations with the goals of the organization.

Here are some practical approaches to inspiring and motivating your team:

1. Clear Vision and Purpose: An authentic leader communicates a clear vision for the team and the organization's purpose. When team members understand the 'why' behind their work, it becomes a source of motivation. It's not just a job; it's a meaningful contribution.

2. Acknowledge and Appreciate: Authentic leaders regularly acknowledge and appreciate the efforts and achievements of their team. This recognition can be as simple as a genuine 'thank you' or a more elaborate appreciation program. It's about making people feel valued.

3. Encourage Growth and Development: Authentic leaders are invested in the growth and development of their team members. They provide opportunities for learning, offer guidance, and create an environment that fosters personal and professional development.

4. Foster Inclusivity: An inclusive environment where every team member's voice is heard and respected is a motivating one. Authentic leaders ensure that all team members feel like they belong and that their contributions are valued.

5. Lead by Example: Authentic leaders don't ask their team to do something they wouldn't do themselves. They lead by example, demonstrating the values, work ethic, and commitment they expect from their team.

Mindful leadership isn't about grandstanding or wearing a badge of honor. It's about showing up authentically, being transparent, building trust through consistent actions, and inspiring and motivating teams through practical strategies. When you lead with authenticity and mindfulness, you're creating a foundation of trust, credibility, and motivation. Your team will recognize and appreciate your authenticity, and in return, you'll find yourself with a motivated, engaged, and committed group of individuals ready to work together towards common goals.

9.2: Mindful Decision-Making in Leadership

In the field of leadership, the capacity to make impactful decisions is not merely a valuable trait; it's the essence of effective leadership. Decisions are the groundwork that become foundation of leadership, and the quality of those threads determines the strength and resilience of the leadership. As a leader, you're constantly faced with choices that can shape the future of your team, your organization, and your own career. How do you make decisions that stand the test of time and create positive ripples?

In this sub-chapter, we'll delve into the art of mindful decision-making in leadership. We'll explore practical methods that empower leaders to navigate the complexities of decision-making with clarity and confidence. No hocus-pocus, no guesswork, just grounded strategies that have been proven time and again.

Practical Methods for Impactful Decision-Making through Mindfulness

Mindfulness, in the context of decision-making, is your compass through uncharted waters. It's the steady hand guiding you as you navigate the swirling currents of options and consequences. Being mindful means being fully present in the moment, aware of your thoughts and emotions without judgment. When you approach decision-making with mindfulness, you're more attuned to your intuition, values, and the needs of your team.

Practical Method 1: The Pause

One of the simplest yet most effective methods for impactful decision-making is the art of the pause. When faced with a critical decision, give yourself the gift of time. Take a breath, step back, and let your thoughts settle. Rushing into decisions often leads to impulsivity, whereas a mindful pause allows you to see the bigger picture. It permits you to assess not just the immediate implications but also the long-term effects. Think of it as zooming out on the decision canvas. Ask yourself, "What is the core purpose of this decision? What are the potential ramifications? How does it align with our values and goals?" The pause is not a delay; it's a strategic move that prevents hasty, regrettable choices.

Practical Method 2: The Mindful Scan

The mindful scan is your tool for assessing your own biases and preconceptions. We all have them; it's part of being human. But effective leaders acknowledge their biases and aim to make decisions based on impartial assessment. The mindful scan involves systematically examining your thoughts and emotions related to a decision. It's an internal audit, an interrogation of your own thinking. Are you making this choice because it's the best path, or because it's the easiest? Are you influenced by fear, ego, or external pressures? This method encourages a conscious shift from emotional reactions to rational evaluations, ensuring your decisions are grounded in objective wisdom.

Practical Method 3: The Power of Silence

Amid the noise of daily leadership, the power of silence often goes unnoticed. In decision-making, silence can be your ally. When you're considering an important choice, practice the discipline of silence. Listen to what others have to say. Invite different perspectives, even conflicting ones. Let your team and colleagues share their insights. Be fully present during these conversations, not as the person with the answers but as someone open to the collective wisdom. Silence doesn't mean indecision; it means humility, an acknowledgment that the best decisions often emerge from the collaboration of minds.

Navigating Leadership Challenges and Conflicts with a Clear Mind

Leadership isn't a solitary journey through calm seas; it's a voyage through turbulent waters, and challenges are the tempests that test your mettle. Decision-making during challenging times requires a steadfast, clear mind. It's here that the fusion of mindfulness and practicality becomes most critical.

Practical Method 4: The Solution-Centered Approach

In the face of challenges and conflicts, it's easy to become overwhelmed by the gravity of the situation. But mindful leaders embrace a solution-centered approach. They acknowledge the problem, yet they don't dwell on it. Instead, they direct their focus toward solutions. How can we resolve this? What steps can we take to navigate this challenge? Mindfulness helps in maintaining a clear, focused mindset amid chaos. It keeps you from being engulfed by the problem and guides you toward actionable solutions.

Practical Method 5: Constructive Feedback Loop

A clear mind is open to feedback. Conflicts and challenges often arise due to miscommunication or unmet expectations. Mindful leaders create a feedback loop that encourages open dialogue. They seek input from their team and colleagues, fostering an environment where concerns can be addressed constructively. Constructive feedback allows leaders to make informed decisions based on the actual needs and perceptions of those involved. It's a practical approach that prevents misunderstandings from turning into conflicts.

Leadership Success through Proven Decision-Making Strategies

Success in leadership is not defined by the absence of mistakes but by the ability to learn from them. Proven decision-making strategies are the cornerstones of effective leadership. They are the tools that enable you to make decisions that contribute to your team's growth and your organization's success.

Practical Method 6: Scenario Analysis

Scenario analysis is a practical strategy that involves considering various potential outcomes of a decision. It's like playing chess, thinking several moves ahead. When faced with a complex decision, mindful leaders explore different scenarios. What if we choose Path A? What are the likely consequences, and how can we mitigate risks? What if we opt for Path B? By anticipating possible outcomes, you're better equipped to make decisions that account for multiple contingencies.

Practical Method 7: The 10-10-10 Rule

The 10-10-10 rule is a pragmatic tool for evaluating the long-term impact of a decision. It's a lens through which you examine how a decision will affect you, your team, and your organization in ten minutes, ten months, and ten years. It encourages leaders to consider not just short-term gains but also the sustainability and consequences of their choices. It's a method that ensures you're not just seeking success now but also setting a course for long-term leadership excellence.

Mindful decision-making in leadership is about making framework of clarity, wisdom, and practicality. It's an art that requires practice and patience. By incorporating practical methods into your leadership approach and combining them with mindfulness, you're better equipped to make decisions that not only stand the test but benefitted all party.

9.3: Leading Through Change with Mindfulness

In the professional world, change is not merely a constant; it's the new norm. Whether it's a shift in market dynamics, an organizational restructuring, or a complete pivot in business strategy, change is an inescapable facet of modern leadership. However, it's how leaders manage and guide their teams through these transformations that truly sets the course for success or stagnation. This chapter delves into the intricate process of leading through change with mindfulness and practical leadership strategies.

Managing Teams during Organizational Changes with Mindfulness

The tides of change can evoke a spectrum of emotions in any organization - anxiety, resistance, uncertainty. As a leader, your role is akin to that of a captain navigating a ship through turbulent waters. Mindfulness becomes your compass, grounding you in the present moment while acknowledging the emotional tempest surrounding you.

The cornerstone of managing teams during organizational changes is effective communication. In times of upheaval, silence can be more destructive than discord. Start by acknowledging the change and its impact on your team. Openly address questions and concerns, fostering a space where apprehensions can be shared without fear of judgment.

Mindfulness encourages empathetic listening - a skill that can defuse tensions and build bridges between leaders and their teams. Truly hearing your team's perspectives, fears, and suggestions is a mindful practice that often elicits innovative solutions. It's not about having all the answers; it's about having the humility to accept that you don't.

While navigating change, it's vital to convey a clear vision of the future. With mindfulness, you can anchor this vision in the present, illuminating a path forward amidst the uncertainty. Clearly articulate how each team member fits into this new vision. Mindfulness teaches us to remain flexible and adapt to the evolving landscape, and this adaptability can be a beacon of hope for your team.

Practical leadership during change also requires self-awareness. Your emotional state is contagious, and your team will mirror your demeanor. Mindfulness equips you to manage your own emotions and stay composed in the face of turmoil. This composure can be a wellspring of strength for your team, reassuring them that, though the winds are tempestuous, the ship will remain steady.

Practical Strategies for Guiding Teams Through Transitions

Change is an combination of uncertainty and adaptation, and leading through it demands a choreography of practical strategies. One such strategy is the creation of a roadmap. Visualize your destination and chart a clear, practical path towards it. Break down the transformation into manageable milestones, providing your team with a sense of structure and progress.

Moreover, involve your team in the change process. Seek their input on how to implement the changes effectively. By involving them, you not only gather valuable insights but also foster a sense of ownership over the transformation. It's no longer "the organization's change"; it becomes "our change."

Change can be disorienting, and as a leader, you're the compass that guides your team's sense of direction. Clarity is your most potent tool. Communicate the goals, the tactics, and the progress. And remember that repetition is key. People need to hear information multiple times to truly absorb it.

Practical leadership also demands the allocation of resources and support. Ensure your team has the tools and training they need to succeed in the new landscape. Acknowledge their efforts and provide continuous feedback. This not only motivates your team but also keeps you connected to their individual experiences.

Empowering Teams to Embrace Change Using Proven Leadership Techniques

Empowering your team to embrace change is a testament to your leadership skills. The journey towards change can be daunting, but you, as the leader, are the torchbearer, illuminating the path forward. Your team's transition can be eased through the consistent application of proven leadership techniques.

First and foremost, lead by example. Model the behaviors, attitudes, and work ethic you expect from your team. Embrace change yourself, and your team will likely follow suit. Mindfulness teaches you to be present and adaptable, demonstrating that change isn't insurmountable but a part of growth.

Furthermore, foster a culture of adaptability. Encourage experimentation and risk-taking. A team that isn't afraid to make mistakes is a team that will innovate. Emphasize the importance of learning from setbacks. As a mindful leader, you appreciate that growth often occurs through adversity, and this mindset can be infectious.

It's vital to recognize and celebrate small wins during the change process. By doing so, you reinforce the idea that progress is happening, even if it's gradual. Acknowledge individual and team achievements, no matter how minor. This validation bolsters morale and reinforces the path forward.

Lastly, promote collaboration and open communication. A culture of collaboration encourages collective problem-solving and brainstorming. Mindfulness can facilitate this by fostering an environment where each team member feels heard and valued. When people feel connected and appreciated, their resistance to change is often diminished.

Leading through change with mindfulness and practical strategies is akin to steering a ship through tumultuous seas. It necessitates empathetic communication, self-awareness, clear direction, and the empowerment of your team. Mindful leader duty is to guiding his team toward success.

Change may be daunting, but with the right approach, it becomes a pathway to growth and transformation.

Chapter 10: Mindful Networking and Practical Networking Skills

10.1: Mindful Networking Strategies

In the realm of professional success, one often overlooked but profoundly influential tool is networking. Networking, when approached mindfully, can be a game-changer in your career. It's not about collecting business cards like trophies or engaging in meaningless small talk at conferences. Instead, it's about building authentic, meaningful connections that are driven by intention, and rooted in the authenticity of your professional self. In this subchapter, we will delve into mindful networking strategies, exploring how to build connections that matter, how to approach networking with intention and authenticity, and how to enhance your professional reputation through proven networking skills.

Building Meaningful Connections Through Practical Networking Techniques

Networking isn't just about who you know; it's about the quality and depth of the relationships you nurture. Meaningful connections can open doors, offer support, and lead to opportunities that you might not have anticipated. The key is to focus on building relationships that go beyond the superficial. Here are practical networking techniques to help you do just that:

1. Be Curious and Ask Questions: When engaging in networking events or conversations, curiosity is your most

valuable asset. Ask open-ended questions that invite others to share their experiences and insights. Show a genuine interest in what they have to say. This approach not only helps you learn from others but also establishes a strong foundation for a meaningful connection.

2. Active Listening: Active listening is a cornerstone of mindful networking. It involves being fully present in the moment, giving your undivided attention to the person you're speaking with, and seeking to understand their perspective. When you listen actively, you show respect for the other person's thoughts and experiences, and you create a space where meaningful connections can flourish.

3. Add Value: Networking is a two-way street. To build meaningful connections, focus on adding value to others. This can be as simple as sharing a relevant article, offering to introduce them to someone in your network, or helping them solve a problem. By being a source of value, you become a valuable connection yourself.

Networking with Intention and Authenticity
Networking with intention means that every connection you make serves a purpose. It's not about the quantity of connections but the quality of those connections and how they align with your career goals and values. Here's how to network with intention and authenticity:

1. Define Your Goals: Before diving into networking, take a step back and define your objectives. What do you hope to achieve through networking? Whether it's finding a

mentor, exploring job opportunities, or learning from industry experts, clarity in your goals will guide your networking efforts.

2. Identify Your Core Values: Authenticity in networking stems from aligning your actions with your core values. When your networking efforts align with what you truly value, it's easier to establish genuine connections. Identify what's important to you in your professional life and make sure your network reflects those values.

3. Craft Your Elevator Pitch: When introducing yourself, be clear, concise, and authentic. Your elevator pitch should convey who you are, what you do, and what you're passionate about. Authenticity in your pitch sets the tone for a meaningful exchange.

Enhancing Your Professional Reputation Through Proven Networking Skills

Your professional reputation is a valuable asset that can be enhanced through mindful networking. Reputation matters, as it influences how others perceive you and whether they trust and respect you. To improve your professional reputation through networking, consider these proven networking skills:

1. Reliability: Being reliable and delivering on your promises is key to building a positive reputation. When you follow through on commitments and meet deadlines, others view you as dependable and trustworthy.

2. Communication Skills: Effective communication is at the heart of successful networking. Practice clear, respectful, and thoughtful communication, both in person and online. Your ability to articulate your thoughts and listen to others will contribute to a favorable reputation.

3. Consistency: Consistency in your interactions and behavior is vital for reputation management. People need to know what to expect from you, and they should consistently experience professionalism and authenticity in your interactions.

In the world of networking, it's not just about who you know, but who knows you and what they think of you. Building meaningful connections, networking with intention and authenticity, and enhancing your professional reputation are all interconnected aspects of mindful networking. When you approach networking with these strategies in mind, you'll not only expand your professional network but also deepen your connections, and enhance your career prospects.

10.2: Online Networking with Mindfulness

In our rapidly evolving digital age, the landscape of networking has transformed. The traditional ways of shaking hands at conferences or local meet-ups now coexist with the vast realm of online networking. The digital space, with its array of social media platforms, professional networking websites, and virtual communities, offers us unprecedented opportunities to connect with professionals from all corners of the globe. The question is, how do we leverage these online platforms effectively? How can we craft a compelling online presence? And most importantly, how do we build and nurture meaningful relationships in the virtual world? These questions are central to your online networking journey, and in this subchapter, we'll explore practical steps to navigate the complex yet rewarding realm of online networking.

Leveraging Online Platforms for Effective Networking

Online networking isn't a mere extension of traditional networking; it's an entirely different realm with its own rules and nuances. It's a world where the power of the written word and the impact of digital interactions can be harnessed to forge meaningful connections.

Let's start by emphasizing the importance of selecting the right platforms. You wouldn't go to a professional conference unrelated to your field, and similarly, your online presence should be strategically targeted. LinkedIn, for instance, is a powerhouse for professional networking. It's the virtual equivalent of a networking event filled with professionals from diverse industries. If you're a creative professional, platforms like Behance or Dribbble can showcase your work. Consider the nature of your field and your networking goals, and choose your online platforms accordingly.

Once you're in the right space, engage thoughtfully. Share relevant content, comment on posts, and connect with professionals who inspire you. It's not about collecting connections like trophies; it's about building relationships. Send personalized connection requests with a brief introduction. Remember, it's a digital handshake, and your message should convey your intent to connect meaningfully.

Building a Strong Online Presence with Practical Steps

Your online presence is your digital fingerprint. It's the impression you leave on professionals who come across your profile. Much like a well-constructed resume or an eloquent elevator pitch, your online presence should tell a compelling story. Start with your profile picture. It's your digital first impression, so opt for a professional and approachable photo. Your headline should succinctly convey who you are and what you're passionate about.

In your summary section, go beyond the generic buzzwords. Share your story, your professional journey, and what motivates you. Remember, authenticity shines brighter than clichés. It's not about what you do but why you do it. An example:

"As a marketing strategist, I'm driven by the pursuit of creative solutions that help brands connect with their audiences on a deeper level. My journey in this ever-evolving field has taught me the value of innovative thinking and the art of storytelling."

The experience section should be a detailed resume of your career. Each role should paint a picture of your accomplishments and the skills you've honed. Use action words, quantify achievements, and showcase the value you've added to your previous roles. Your connections and potential employers want to see not only where you've been but where you're headed.

Maximizing the Impact of Virtual Connections through Proven Online Networking Strategies

The virtual world offers endless possibilities, but the key to success lies in strategic networking. Much like face-to-face networking, it's essential to have a clear purpose. Are you seeking job opportunities, mentorship, or collaboration on a project? Defining your objectives will guide your interactions.

Let's talk about content sharing. It's not enough to have an impressive profile; you must also contribute meaningfully. Share articles, posts, or even write your own content on subjects that resonate with your field. Position yourself as a thought leader by providing valuable insights. When you add value to your network, you become a go-to resource.

Maintaining and Nurturing Professional Relationships

Building connections in the online world is just the beginning. The true power of your network lies in the relationships you foster. The adage "out of sight, out of mind" is particularly relevant here. Maintaining and nurturing professional relationships requires consistent effort.

After connecting with someone, send a thank-you message or an introduction to initiate a conversation. Engage in online discussions and groups relevant to your field. Respond promptly to messages and connection requests. The more you give in terms of time and knowledge, the more you'll receive in return.

Also, don't underestimate the significance of offline interactions. Whenever possible, consider meeting your online connections in person. Attend industry events, conferences, or even arrange informal meet-ups. These face-to-face encounters solidify your online relationships and take them to a deeper level.

The online networking world is vast, ever-evolving, and offers endless opportunities for career growth. By thoughtfully leveraging online platforms, constructing a compelling online presence, following practical networking steps, and nurturing relationships, you can harness the power of online networking to advance your career and achieve your professional goals. Remember, networking isn't a one-time event; it's a journey that continues to unfold as you engage, connect, and grow in the virtual space.

Chapter 11: Mindfulness in Interviews, Presentations, and Practical Techniques

11.1: Mindful Interview Preparation

Interviews can be nerve-wracking. Whether it's the promising opening for your dream job or a stepping stone in your career journey, the mere thought of stepping into that room, or these days, that virtual meeting, can stir a complex mix of emotions - anticipation, self-doubt, and, occasionally, sheer dread. Interviews are the stage where we're not just under the spotlight but are, in essence, the spotlight itself. In the world of career advancement, interviews represent a critical turning point. However, with mindfulness and practical steps, you can not only survive but also thrive in these high-pressure situations.

Preparing Confidently for Interviews with Practical Steps

Confidence is the golden ticket to a successful interview. It's what transforms your qualifications on paper into a compelling presence in the room or on the screen. Building confidence through mindfulness is like constructing a sturdy bridge that takes you from self-doubt to self-assuredness.

Start by understanding the components of your self-doubt. What are the thoughts that make your heart race, palms sweat, and stomach churn? It might be the fear of not knowing how to respond to a tricky question or the idea that you're underqualified. These are the shaky planks on your bridge. Mindfulness teaches you to observe these thoughts without judgment. Picture them as passing clouds in the vast sky of your mind. They come and go, but they don't define you. This mental shift is the foundational step to building confidence.

Practical Steps:

1. Grounding Breaths: Before the interview, find a quiet space. Close your eyes and take a few deep breaths. Feel your feet on the ground. Let the sensation of your body's contact with the earth anchor you in the present moment. With each breath, release the tension in your body and the doubts in your mind.

2. Positive Visualization: Mindfulness invites you to visualize success, not failure. Close your eyes and picture the interview. See yourself answering questions with poise and confidence. Visualize the interviewer nodding in approval. This positive mental rehearsal fosters a sense of readiness and assurance.

3. Affirmations: Use affirmations to boost your confidence. Phrases like "I am well-prepared" or "I am qualified for this position" can work wonders. Recite them as part of your mindfulness practice, emphasizing the truth in these statements. Over time, they become your inner armor.

Mindful Interview Research and Preparation Strategies

Preparation is the key to confidence. You've done your grounding exercises, and now it's time to delve into the practical aspect of interview preparation. You're not just walking into the interview room; you're walking in with a toolbelt of skills and knowledge that will help you navigate the conversation with ease.

Research is the cornerstone of interview preparation. It's about understanding your potential employer, their values, their mission, and their needs. The aim is not just to know about the company but to resonate with it. Mindfulness comes into play here as it encourages you to approach research with a curious and non-judgmental attitude.

Instead of viewing research as a tedious task, see it as an opportunity to learn. Approach it with an open mind. Read about the company's journey, its culture, and its recent accomplishments. What values do they hold dear, and how do those values align with your own? This is where the magic of mindful research happens.

Practical Steps:

1. Company Website: Start with the company's website. Explore sections like the 'About Us' and 'Mission and Values.' Pay attention to their success stories, their culture, and their commitment to social and environmental responsibilities.

2. News and Articles: Dive into news articles and publications related to the company. What recent projects or achievements have they been part of? How have they contributed to their industry and community?

3. LinkedIn: Visit the LinkedIn profiles of current employees, especially those in the department or role you're

interviewing for. What can you learn about their backgrounds and the paths that led them to the company?

Proven Techniques for Succeeding in Interviews

Now that you've grounded yourself and immersed in mindful research, it's time to master the art of answering interview questions. There's a multitude of potential questions, but they typically fall into common categories: your background, your qualifications, your problem-solving abilities, and your fit with the company's culture.

Mindfulness can transform these questions from intimidating interrogations into opportunities for authentic self-expression. The essence of mindfulness is presence. It's about being fully engaged in the current moment. In the context of an interview, this translates into active listening.

Proven Techniques:

1. Listening Closely: Instead of rehearsing answers while the interviewer speaks, truly listen. It's a moment of connection and understanding. Feel the words as they are spoken, and let your responses flow naturally from this place of presence.

2. The Pause: Silence is not your enemy; it's your ally. When you're asked a question, take a moment to collect your thoughts. This pause is your sanctuary of mindfulness. It allows you to respond thoughtfully rather than impulsively.

3. Storytelling: Share your experiences in the form of stories. Stories are memorable, relatable, and engaging. They allow you to showcase your skills and qualifications in a way that resonates with the interviewer.

Remember that interviews are not just about proving your qualifications. They are also an opportunity for the company to discover if you are the right fit for their culture. This is where your mindful research becomes invaluable. You can articulate how your values align with the company's, how your experiences have shaped your professional journey, and how you envision contributing to the company's mission.

The process of mindful interview preparation is not just about winning the interview; it's about aligning your authentic self with your career aspirations. It's a practice of self-discovery, self-acceptance, and self-confidence. When you enter the interview room with mindfulness, you're not just answering questions; you're engaging in a meaningful conversation, and this shift in perspective can change the trajectory of your career.

11.2: Delivering Impactful Presentations

In the world of professional growth and career advancement, the ability to deliver impactful presentations can be a true game-changer. Whether it's sharing a project proposal, pitching a new idea, or addressing a room full of colleagues, delivering persuasive presentations is a skill that can set you apart from the rest. Yet, for many, the very thought of standing in front of an audience can induce anxiety and doubt. It's a common sentiment, one that often hinders the full realization of our potential. But fear not; we're going to explore practical approaches to overcome public speaking anxiety, deliver persuasive presentations, and build the confidence needed to become an effective public speaker.

Overcoming Public Speaking Anxiety with Practical Approaches

Let's face it: public speaking anxiety is a pervasive fear. For some, the mere idea of stepping onto a stage can trigger a rush of anxiety. The palms get sweaty, the heart races, and thoughts become jumbled. It's as if we're walking into a battlefield, rather than onto a platform. Yet, it's crucial to remember that anxiety is a natural response. It's our body's way of preparing us for action, and it can indeed be managed. The practical approaches to overcoming public speaking anxiety aren't about eradicating it but rather managing it effectively.

Preparation and Familiarity: One of the most effective ways to conquer public speaking anxiety is through preparation. The more you know your material, the more confident you become. Consider your presentation as a story you know inside and out. Your slides, your talking points – they should all be as familiar as your favorite book. When you're comfortable with your material, it's easier to control your anxiety.

Practice: There's a reason they say practice makes perfect. Rehearsing your presentation multiple times can help reduce anxiety. Stand in front of a mirror, record yourself, or better yet, practice in front of a friend or family member. Feedback from others can be invaluable.

Mindfulness Techniques: Mindfulness, a practice that encourages living in the present moment, can also be a powerful tool in overcoming public speaking anxiety. By grounding yourself in the now, you can manage your anxious thoughts. Before your presentation, take a few minutes to breathe deeply, center yourself, and remind yourself that this moment is the only moment that matters.

Visualization: Picture yourself delivering a successful presentation. Visualization is a powerful technique used by athletes, and it can work just as effectively for public speakers. When you imagine yourself succeeding, your mind begins to believe in the possibility.

Delivering Persuasive Presentations through Proven Methods

Once you've tackled your anxiety, the next step is delivering persuasive presentations. Persuasion is a nuanced art, one that combines logic and emotion, data and storytelling. Your presentation isn't just about disseminating information; it's about convincing your audience of your perspective. Here are some proven methods to make your presentations more persuasive.

Know Your Audience: Effective persuasion begins with understanding your audience. Who are they? What are their concerns, desires, and motivations? Tailor your message to resonate with your listeners.

Storytelling: Human beings are naturally drawn to stories. Incorporate anecdotes and narratives into your presentation to connect with your audience on a deeper level. Stories can make your message relatable and memorable.

Clear Structure: A well-structured presentation is a persuasive one. Ensure your presentation has a clear beginning, middle, and end. Start with an engaging introduction, provide supporting details in the body, and conclude with a strong call to action or key takeaways.

Visual Aids: Visual aids, such as slides or props, can enhance your message. Use them strategically to reinforce your points and make complex information more digestible.

Engage with Emotion: While data and facts are essential, don't neglect the emotional aspect of persuasion. People are often moved more by emotions than statistics. Share personal stories, use powerful language, and tap into the emotional side of your audience.

Building Confidence and Effectiveness as a Public Speaker with Practical Skills

Confidence as a public speaker is a journey, not a destination. It's an ongoing process of self-discovery and self-improvement. Building confidence comes from both practice and mindset shifts.

Positive Self-Talk: The words we tell ourselves can shape our reality. Instead of dwelling on what could go wrong, focus on what could go right. Replace negative self-talk with positive affirmations. Tell yourself, "I am a confident and capable speaker."

Feedback and Improvement: Seek feedback from trusted sources to identify areas for improvement. Constructive criticism can be a valuable tool for enhancing your skills. Use it as an opportunity for growth, not as a personal critique.

Public Speaking Courses: Consider enrolling in public speaking courses or workshops. These environments offer a safe space to practice and refine your skills, while professional guidance can help you make significant strides in your public speaking journey.

Record and Review: Record your presentations and review them objectively. Pay attention to your body language, vocal tone, and pacing. This allows you to identify areas that need improvement and track your progress.

Becoming an effective public speaker is a transformative process. It begins with acknowledging and managing your anxiety, progresses to delivering persuasive presentations, and culminates in building confidence and effectiveness. With practical approaches and consistent effort, you can not only conquer public speaking anxiety but also become a persuasive and confident public speaker, ready to leave your mark in the world of professional growth and career advancement.

11.3: Handling Rejections and Feedback Mindfully

Rejection stings. No matter how seasoned or confident we are, hearing "no" can still bruise our pride and shake our confidence. But in the ever-evolving landscape of our careers, rejection is an unavoidable visitor. If we choose to see it not as an adversary but as a mentor, we might just discover that it holds valuable lessons for our professional and personal growth.

In the process of navigating interviews and presentations, we encounter countless moments where our hopes and ambitions collide with the harsh reality of rejection. Each rejection is, in essence, an invitation—an invitation to practice mindfulness and learn from the experience. Here, in this subchapter, we will delve into the art of handling rejection mindfully, using it as a stepping stone to personal and career growth.

Coping with Rejection and Learning from It with Practical Strategies

Let's begin by acknowledging that coping with rejection is a deeply human experience. It's natural to feel disappointment, frustration, and even a touch of self-doubt when our best efforts are met with a "no" or a closed door. What's important is how we respond to these emotions.

Mindfulness teaches us to approach rejection with self-compassion. Instead of berating ourselves for not being good enough, we can recognize that rejection often stems from a complex interplay of factors, many of which are beyond our control. It's not a reflection of our worth as individuals.

One practical strategy for coping with rejection mindfully is to engage in self-reflection. Take a step back and assess the situation objectively. Were there areas where you could improve? Were there aspects beyond your control? Rather than dwelling on the negative emotions, channel your energy into a constructive analysis.

Using Feedback for Personal and Career Growth with Practical Steps

Feedback is a powerful tool for personal and career growth, and yet, it's often underutilized. When we receive feedback, especially constructive criticism, we have a choice: to react defensively or to accept it as an opportunity for improvement.

Mindfulness encourages us to embrace feedback with an open heart and an open mind. Instead of viewing it as a personal attack, consider it a valuable insight into your performance. Whether it's feedback from an interviewer, a colleague, or a mentor, each piece of feedback can be seen as a potential gift.

Practical steps to utilize feedback include actively seeking it out. Don't wait for feedback to come to you; ask for it. During interviews and presentations, inquire about your performance, and request honest assessments. This not only demonstrates your commitment to improvement but also provides you with immediate insights for adjustment.

Furthermore, when feedback arrives, avoid the temptation to react impulsively. Take time to digest it. Consider its validity and its potential for enhancing your skills. Instead of defending your actions, ask yourself, "How can I use this feedback to become better at what I do?"

Building Resilience through Mindfulness and Practical Feedback Utilization

Resilience is the ability to bounce back from adversity. It's a quality that distinguishes those who thrive in the face of challenges from those who crumble under pressure. Building resilience isn't an overnight transformation; it's a journey—one that mindfulness can greatly facilitate.

Practical steps to build resilience include reframing your mindset. Instead of viewing rejection as an insurmountable obstacle, view it as a detour on the path to your goals. Understand that many accomplished individuals have faced rejection and emerged stronger because of it.

Mindfulness teaches us to approach challenges with equanimity. By staying present and observing our reactions, we can prevent our emotions from spiraling out of control. This equanimity allows us to face rejection and criticism with composure and grace.

Incorporate mindfulness practices into your daily routine, especially during moments of adversity. These practices can include deep breathing exercises, meditation, or mindful journaling. The key is to anchor yourself in the present moment, allowing you to navigate difficulties with a clearer perspective.

Handling rejection and feedback mindfully is not a one-time effort but a lifelong practice. It's about embracing these experiences as opportunities for growth, not as setbacks. As we become more resilient, compassionate, and open to learning, we transform rejection from an adversary into a mentor, guiding us toward the peak of our careers. Embracing these practical strategies and nurturing a mindful approach can help us not only survive but thrive in the ever-changing world of our professional lives.

Conclusion

As we come to the end of our journey through the pages of this book," I invite you to pause for a moment and reflect on the path you've traveled. The journey to career success is far from linear; it's a dynamic and often unpredictable expedition through uncharted territory. It's a journey that demands courage, vulnerability, and resilience.

Through the course of this book, we've explored the profound intersection of mindfulness, affirmation, and practical career strategies. We've delved into the depths of personal development, honed our communication skills, and learned the art of networking and relationship building. We've embraced the mindful integration of these principles in interviews, presentations, and the hum of everyday professional life.

Now, as we reach this conclusion, it's a moment to anchor ourselves and draw the threads of our career journey together. It's an opportunity to celebrate the ground we've covered and the wisdom we've gathered along the way.

Reflecting on Mindfulness and Affirmations

Mindfulness isn't just about meditation or breathing exercises; it's a way of life. It's a commitment to being present in each moment, to observing our thoughts and emotions, and to embracing the power of conscious awareness. Throughout this book, we've discovered how mindfulness can transform our reactions, choices, and interactions in the workplace.

Affirmations, on the other hand, serve as the mantras of change. They're not mere words; they're the fertile seeds from which self-belief, confidence, and resilience grow. We've explored how crafting and embracing affirmations tailored to your unique career goals can be a game-changer.

But remember, this journey isn't about perfection. Mindfulness and affirmations are tools in your toolbox. They're the compass and the map for your career journey, helping you navigate the sometimes tumultuous waters of the professional world. They won't eliminate challenges, but they'll equip you with the resilience and clarity to face them head-on.

The Dance of Practical Career Strategies

Beyond mindfulness and affirmations, our journey has been enriched by a host of practical career strategies. We've explored effective communication, empathetic leadership, and the art of networking. These are the tangible skills that give you an edge in the working world. They are the rungs on the ladder to career success.

From preparing for interviews to mastering the art of public speaking, we've uncovered the tools and techniques that can make a significant difference in how you present yourself and communicate with others. We've recognized that networking isn't just about accumulating contacts but about nurturing meaningful relationships. We've explored how resilience and adaptability aren't just desirable qualities; they're essential for navigating the ever-evolving career landscape.

Navigating Rejection and Feedback

Throughout your career journey, you'll encounter rejection and feedback, two steadfast companions on the road to success. We've discovered that rejection, rather than a dead-end, can be a pivot point. It's an opportunity for self-reflection, growth, and, ultimately, resilience. We've learned how to handle it mindfully, letting it serve as a mentor rather than an adversary.

Feedback, too, is a gem in your toolkit. It's a source of growth and learning, a reflection of your journey. When approached with an open heart and a willingness to improve, feedback becomes a catalyst for your personal and career development.

Remember that every "no" or constructive criticism isn't a rejection of you as an individual but a stepping stone on your path to excellence. The strength of mindfulness and affirmations lies in their ability to help you embrace these moments with grace and composure.

Embracing Lifelong Learning and Evolution

In closing, let's emphasize the power of lifelong learning and personal evolution. Your career journey doesn't have an end point, but it's an ever-evolving process. It's about setting new goals, expanding your horizons, and striving for continuous improvement.

Mindfulness and affirmations, when embraced as lifelong practices, will accompany you on this journey. They'll help you stay grounded, focused, and self-aware. They'll be your companions in times of triumph and tribulation.

So, as you take the knowledge, insights, and practical strategies from this book into the world, remember that your career is not just a destination but a journey—a journey to the peak of your potential. It's a journey where each step, whether uphill or downhill, contributes to your growth and wisdom.

As we part ways on this written path, remember that your journey is unique. You are the author of your story, the architect of your career, and the artist of your destiny. May you use the wisdom gathered here to build a career that not only reaches its peak but thrives there.

Embrace each moment with the mindfulness and affirmation that you carry, and remember that, in the words of Henry David Thoreau, "Go confidently in the direction of your dreams. Live the life you have imagined." Your peak is not a far-off summit but the very ground beneath your feet. It's where you choose to stand, here and now.

Thank you for read this book. It's been an honor to be your guide.

BONUS

Interview Preparation Checklist
Before the Interview:

- [ ] Research the company, its mission, values, and recent news.

- [ ] Understand the job role and its requirements thoroughly.

- [ ] Review your resume and be ready to discuss your work experience.

- [ ] Prepare specific examples of your accomplishments and skills.

- [ ] Research the role you're interviewing for to anticipate questions.

- [ ] Create a list of questions to ask the interviewer about the company and role.

- [ ] Choose professional attire suitable for the company culture.

- [ ] Plan your route to the interview location and account for potential traffic or delays.

- [ ] Confirm the interview date, time, and location.

What to Bring:

- [ ] Multiple copies of your resume.

- [ ] A notepad and pen for taking notes.

- [ ] Portfolio or work samples, if relevant.

- [ ] A list of professional references.

Day of the Interview:

- [ ] Arrive early but not too early (10-15 minutes before the interview).

- [ ] Be polite and respectful to everyone you meet, from the receptionist to the interviewer.

- [ ] Maintain a positive attitude and confidence.

- [ ] Practice good body language (firm handshake, eye contact, good posture).

- [ ] Listen actively to the interviewer's questions and respond thoughtfully.

- [ ] Use the STAR method (Situation, Task, Action, Result) for behavioral questions.

- [ ] Showcase your soft skills (communication, teamwork, problem-solving).

- [ ] Provide examples of your achievements and how they can benefit the company.

After the Interview:

- [ ] Send a thank-you email within 24 hours expressing appreciation for the opportunity.

- [ ] Reflect on your performance during the interview and note areas for improvement.

- [ ] Follow up on any action items discussed during the interview.

- [ ] Continue your job search and attend other interviews until you have an offer.

General Tips:

- [ ] Stay calm and confident.

- [ ] Practice your responses to common interview questions.

- [ ] Prepare for competency-based questions.

- [ ] Research the company culture to ensure it's a good fit for you.

- [ ] Be honest and genuine in your responses.

- [ ] Communicate your enthusiasm for the role and company.

- [ ] Show appreciation for the opportunity, regardless of the outcome.

Networking and Relationship Building Checklist
Before Networking:

- [ ] Define your networking goals. What do you want to achieve through networking?

- [ ] Research your target audience. Who are the key people in your industry or field?

- [ ] Prepare your elevator pitch. Can you concisely introduce yourself and your objectives?

- [ ] Develop a networking strategy. How will you approach and connect with people?

- [ ] Update your professional online presence, including your LinkedIn profile.

Networking Event Preparation:

- [ ] Choose the right networking events. Are they relevant to your goals and industry?

- [ ] Practice active listening and conversation skills.

- [ ] Set realistic expectations. Networking may not yield immediate results.

- [ ] Bring multiple copies of your business cards or contact information.

- [ ] Dress professionally and appropriately for the event.

During Networking:

- [ ] Approach people with a friendly smile and open body language.

- [ ] Use your elevator pitch to introduce yourself clearly and concisely.

- [ ] Ask open-ended questions to encourage conversation.

- [ ] Listen actively and show genuine interest in others.

- [ ] Exchange contact information with those you connect with.

Building and Nurturing Relationships:

- [ ] Follow up after the event with a thank-you message.

- [ ] Connect on LinkedIn or other relevant platforms.

- [ ] Offer assistance or value to your new contacts when appropriate.

- [ ] Stay in touch regularly, sharing industry news or updates.

- [ ] Look for opportunities to meet in person again.

Online Networking:

- [ ] Regularly share and comment on relevant industry content.

- [ ] Engage in online discussions and groups related to your field.

- [ ] Send personalized connection requests with a brief introduction.

- [ ] Be mindful of your online presence and what you share on social media.

- [ ] Respond promptly to messages and connection requests.

Maintaining Professionalism:

- [ ] Keep your commitments and follow through on promises.

- [ ] Be respectful and considerate of others' time and boundaries.

- [ ] Give credit and recognition where it's due.

- [ ] Avoid controversial or divisive topics when networking.

- [ ] Build a reputation as a reliable and trustworthy contact.

Measuring and Assessing Networking Success:

- [ ] Set specific networking goals and track your progress.

- [ ] Evaluate the quality and relevance of your network connections.

- [ ] Consider the value you've gained from your network.

- [ ] Adjust your networking strategy based on your results.

Remember, effective networking is an ongoing process. Regularly revisiting and adapting your networking strategy will help you build and maintain valuable professional relationships over time.